JACOBITES of 1715
North East Scotland

by

Frances McDonnell

 ISBN 1 899568 17 4

"They shook hands with ruin for what they esteemed the Cause of their King and country."

Robert Burns in a letter to Lady Winifred Maxwell Constable, 16 December 1789

"My Dearest

The hurry we are in and the crowd of Visitants since we came here hinders.   I cannot at present give you a full account of me and fellow-prisoners I   would otherwise.

It is enough to tell you in a general that in our progress to this place we have suffered the most barbarous and inhuman treatment ever was heard of in a Christian Country, and have been exposed in all the townes we have travelled thro' to all the mock pomp and outrage could be offered to Clergyman.   Yet God was with us and has strengthened and upheld us; so that at the time, we are all in good habit and health.   From Aberdeen we came that night to Stonehaven, being each of us on the road guarded by a Dutch soldier, riding two together, who died a long thong of leather to our bits, and hal'd us and drove us as they pleased.

At Stonehaven, after they had kept us a long time upon the Streets, we were shut up altogether into their prison house, a thieves' hole, and were like to be stifled for want of air.   We got in at last some straw and tumbled down together like so many pigs in a hogsty.

I cannot ever forget the kindness of the inhabitants to us who brought us in blankets and clean linen.   Dr Garden and I, who have been inseparable companions in this doleful progresse, lay together in a corner and were easie, and resolved by God's grace to suffer the worst could befall us with ane undaunted courage.

When we came to Montrose about four in the afternoon, we were detained on horseback at the Cross a long long hour ere we were ordered to our jail, the whole town and wondering crowd gazing upon us, some God forgive them laughing and flouting at us, but the greatest part wringing their hands and shedding vollies of tears for us.   At length, tho' they had ane upper prison, we were condemned, as if we had been the worst of malefactors, to a low dungeon, where we were so crowded, that we had scarce room to sit or stand, and no thing allowed us to sit down upon, and a long time before we could have any to clean and sweep the hole.

Saturday, Aprile 7th. - We came at night to Arbroath, where we were yet worse used, thrust into the worst jail I think in the kingdom - twenty one of us in number - a nasty filthy hole where we had nothing to sit upon, but an old bier upon which they carry out prisoners and poor people to the grave.   Here we were kept five long hours ere we could have either meat or drink, though we had fasted all the day.

Yet even here our good God did not forsake us, but stirred up the compassion of a deal of good women who sent us in some bottles of ale and furnished us with bedclothes - particularly we were bound to Dr Burnett's wife's sister, Mrs Reid, who was very kind to us.

Sunday, Aprile 8th. - We travelled to Dundee, and came there about the ringing of the last bell to afternoon preaching.   We were held upon the street a long hour, the .... and derision of the whiggish mob of that town, and at last put in prison, the best I believe in the nation, where we had a large gallerie to walk in, and got in bedding. Here the good women and citizens showed a deal of kindness. I here again turned very unwell and was seized with the most racking fit of the collick, but praised be God, after midnight I turned wonderful easier. Here we stayed Monday all day which rested us.

Tuesday, Aprile 10th. - We travelled to Cupar in Fife and there we met Cupar justice indeed! after a deal of indignities and insulting over us, by the ill natured mob while we waited at the Cross. We were thrust into the nastiest and narrowest vaults imaginable; our troop of prisoners being now become very numerous by the accession of a deal of Angus gentlemen.

Wednesday - We were carried to Kirkcaldy, through all the little towns of Fife on the road as a Rareshow.

Thursday - We crossed the Forth at Kinghorn. About 3 o'clock we landed at Leith, amidst a vast concourse of people, and were forced up on foot to travel from Leith to Edinburgh, driven on like so many sacrifices, allowing us no time to halt for breath. I must say with my crippled leg, I thought I never to have got it done, but to have sunk under it, but God supported and strengthened me. We were brought through Leith Wynd and up the High Street to the Mainguard, the whole town viewing us, a glorious parade and triumphal band, while a great many (more) could hardly be kept from rabbling our guard, at the uncouth and lamentable sight. From the mainguard we were ordered to march back down the Canongate, where a deal of gentlemen came with us were put in prison - others and among them we of the Clergy were, with the gentlemen who voluntarily surrendered, put into Winton House in the Canongate, where we of the Clergy had a room to ourselves, five of us together, high and well aired, with a window to the Fore Street.

We have got in very good bedding and our accommodation here is gentle.

Thus, my dear, I have given you a short account of our progresse how long we may stay here God knows, for reports about us are very various, but it appears we are not like to get out in haste. However I hope all shall be well. God be thanked we are once got out of the hands of Swiss and Dutch. Deliver me and all good men from harrassment as we have suffered from their boisterous officers.

My blessing to you and all my children and loved Parishoners.

Let me hear from you. I am to death yours

Letter from John Alexander, Minister of the Church of Scotland, to his wife.

Jacobites of 1715
North East Scotland

Abercromby, Alexander of Brunston or Brunstone

The Poll Book of 1696 gives Alexander Abercrombie, gentleman in Brunstone, Kinoir, his wife, and Thomas, Elizabeth, and Agnes his children. He survived the Rising of 1715 for many years.

Abercromby, Alexander, younger of Cothal

Son of Thomas Abercromby of Cothal, sometime of Collyhill, in Bourtie, who was brother to Alexander Abercromby of Fetternear, and son of Hector Abercromby of Fetternear and Marjory Gordon of Leicheston, his wife. Born in 1662, he went to Douai in 1677 aged 15, being then called the son of "D. Thomas of Fetterneir and Isobel Bisset of Lessendrum, sister of Fr. George Bisset." He did not become a priest but returned home and is described as "pius et ingeniousus adolescens."

Abercromby, George

Son of Alexander Abercromby of Nether Skeith, Banffshire. One of the sixteen heritors of Banffshire who surrendered at Banff in March 1716.

Abercromby, Sir James of Birkenbog

Born 1669 eldest son of Sir Alexander Abercromby and Elizabeth Baird.

Abercromby, Sir James, Bart. of Birkenbog

Second baronet of Birkenbog, being the eldest son of Sir Alexander and his third wife, Elizabeth, daughter of Sir James Baird of Auchmedden. Sir James Abercromby, born about 1669, was MP for Banffshire from 1693 to 1702. He married Mary, daughter of Arthur Gordon of Straloch, and dying in September 1734 was succeeded by his third son Robert.

Abercromby, John, of the Skeith family

Very little is known about him, not even the names of his parents. All that is certain is that Mar was joined in Perth on 4 Oct 1715 by Lachlan, 20th chief of Mackintosh with a regiment raised mostly from his own clan, in which "J.A. of the Skeith family" was one of his lieutenants, his ADC. (He may have been the same man as JA who on 29 June 1716 was, as "a rebel," put on board the ship *Elizabeth and Anne* at Liverpool, for Virginia).

Abercromby, John, of Authorsk (Aquhorsk or Afforsk)

Was the second son of Alexander of Fetternear, by his wife, Jean Seton of Newark, born 1655. His elder brother was Francis

Abercromby of Fetternear, created Lord Glasford, and the younger was Patrick, author of the *Martial Achievements of the Scottish Nation*.

Abercromby, Patrick, Dr

Author of *Martial Achievements of the Scottish Nation*, was the third son of Alexander Abercromby of Fetternear and his wife, Jean Seton, and was born in 1656. At the age of fourteen he was sent to Douai and spent much of his youth at foreign Universities. Took his degree as Doctor of Medicine at St Andrews in 1685 and appointed physician to James II.

Abercromby, Stewart

A clergyman's son. He came to an untimely end as outlined by a letter written by John Alexander, the painter, from Rome, dated 17 August 1718. "Mr Hay, a painter, lately arrived here, confirmed the ill news, which I suppose you know, of poor Stewart Abercromby, the Episcopal Minister's son, who was hanged at Edinburgh for having killed a man in warm blood, the quarrel, as I hear, being for the reputation of Stewart's wife, whom he had but lately married. I suppose it went harder with him, he being concerned in the last affair in Scotland for the King. I wish he had died then of the wounds received for our Master."

Aberdeen, Alexander, of Cairnbulg, Merchant, Aberdeen

Second son of Andrew Aberdeen, merchant in Aberdeen, made burgess on 8 September 1673. Married Elspet, sister of John Ross of Clochan and Arnage. Their eldest son, Alexander, born 1710 was Provost of Aberdeen in 1742.

Abernethy, John, of Mayen

Eldest son of Alexander Abernethy, 1st of Mayen, and his wife, Isobel Hacket, whose family had previously owned the estate. John married Jean, daughter of James Moir, 2nd of Stoneywood by his first wife, Mary Scroggie, and had two daughters, Jean and Elizabeth, and a son, James, 3rd of Mayen, who married Jane Duff of Hatton, and having shot John Leith of Leithhall in Aberdeen in 1763, was outlawed and fled to France where he was visited by Lord Fife in 1766.

Aboyne, John, 3rd Earl of

Son of Charles, 2nd Earl of Aboyne, and his wife, Elizabeth Lyon, second daughter of Patrick, 3rd Earl of Strathmore and Kinghorn.

Achmoutie, Captain John

Had a Commission in the French service in 1692, and a MS at Avignon mentions "Le Capitaine Auchmooty, prisonier a Edimbourg 7 Avril 1716".

Achmoutie, Patrick, servant to the Earl Marischal

"He surrendered his arms and accoutrements to Lord Edward Murray, Deputy Liet. of the County of Perth, upon the proclamation but is now a prisoner and is past 60 years of age."

Adie, David, Merchant, Aberdeen

Son of David Adie, styled "of Newark" and Easter Echt, and his wife, Katherine, daughter of David Skene, half-brother of Sir George Skene of Fintray, young David was also great-grandson of George Jamesone, the artist, his grandmother being the latter's daughter.

Ainslie, Patrick
> Servant to Mary Duncan, in the Mains of Kildrummy, was one of a party taken near Burntisland by the Dutch when they were fetching coal on 11 January 1716.

Ainslie, William of Blackhill

Alexander, Alexander, Writer in Edinburgh

Alexander, John, Painter
> Marjorie Jameson, daughter of George Jameson, "the Socttish Vandyck," married John Alexander, advocate, Edinburgh and John Alexander, the artist born about 1690, was their son.

Alexander, The Rev John, Church of Scotland Minister of Kildrummy
> Obtained degree at St Andrews in 1661. Married Anna Gordon and had two daughters and one son, John. He died in August 1717 aged about 76, and was buried in Kildrummy.

Allardyce, John, Merchant and Provost of Aberdeen
> Called "John Allardes" in most of the Records. Was Provost of Aberdeen for three terms of two years each, the dates of his election being 1700, 1708 and 1712; the first Parliament of Queen Anne and what proved to be the *last* Scottish Parliament, 1703-1707. Son of John "Allardes," merchant burgess of Aberdeen (died 3 Dec 1699, aged 99), and his wife, Isobel Walker, who died in 1680, aged 83. Married firstly to Agnes Mercer, who died 21 Aug 1700 aged 41 and secondly to Jean Smart, who survived the Provost and died 29 Nov 1722, aged 45, aged 60.

Anderson, Alexander, Aberdeen
> Known as "Skipper Anderson", eldest son of Captain John Anderson of Bourtie, who died in 1673. Had five children and died before 1728.

Anderson, Alexander, of Arradoull
> Son of James Anderson, sometime of Auchinreath. Said to have married Anne, daughter of Sir John Gordon of Park, by his third wife, Katherine Ogilvie of Kempcairn, and died in 1727, being at that time practically bankrupt.

Arbuthnot, Thomas, of Peterhead and of Rora 1715 & 1745
> Born in 1681, eldest son of Nathaniel Arbuthnot in Auchlee, Longside, and Elspet Duncan. Married Christian, daughter of William Young, merchant of Peterhead, and had three sons, James, the eldest, born in 1710, and seven daughters. Died 24 March 1762, aged 81.

Arbuthnot, Alexander, Dyer, Peterhead
> Brother of Thomas Arbuthnot of Peterhead and of Rora, born in 1687. Married twice, first to Anna, daughter of James Ogilvie of Boyne, and secondly to Mary, daughter of Alexander Scott of Auchtydonald.

Baird, William, of Auchmedden
> Son of James Baird, younger of Auchmedden, and his wife, Lady Katherine Hay, daughter of George, 2nd Earl of Kinnoull. This James, who died of smallpox in 1681, was eldest son of Sir James Baird, Knight of Auchmedden, and Christian, only daughter of Sir Walter Ogilvie of Boyne.

Bannerman, Sir Alexander, 2nd Bart. of Elsick

Eldest son of Sir Alexander Bannerman, 1st Baronet of Elsick, created by Charles II in 1682. Married in 1699, Isabella, daughter of Sir Donald Macdonald, 3rd Baronet of Sleat, and by her had one son, Alexander, who succeeded to the title, and three daughters. Died in February 1742.

Bannerman, George, brotherof Sir Alexander, 2nd Bart.

Son of Sir Alexander, 1st Baronet of Elsick and his wife Margaret, daughter of Patrick Scott of Thirlestane. George was at Marischal College with his brother Alexander from 1688-92.

Bannerman, Captain John 1715

Described as "Uncle of the Provost," ie Sir Patrick Bannerman. Fourth son of Alexander Bannerman of Elsick by his second marriage.

Bannerman, Mark, first cousin of the Provost

Sir Alexander Bannerman, 1st Baronet of Elsick, had a younger half-brother Robert, Episcopal Minister of Newton (Dalkeith) who was deposed for not praying for William and Mary and for refusing to take the Oath in 1689. He married Margaret, daughter of Sir Mark Carse of Cockpen, and the above Mark was his youngest son.

Bannerman, Sir Patrick, brother of George and Sir Alexander

Fourth son of Sir Alexander Bannerman, he married Margaret, daughter of Sir Charles Maitland of Pitrichie, by whom he had two sons. Died 4 June 1733.

Bisset, James, of Lessendrum

The eldest son of Robert Bisset, 9th of Lessendrum and his wife, Agnes, daughter of Sir Alexander Abercromby, 1st Baronet of Birkenbog. Died in 1748.

Black, Gilbert, Under-Master at the Grammar School, Aberdeen

Son of Gilbert Black, late Baillie, was at Marischal College from 1680-84.

Black, Dr Robert, Physician to Lord Panmure

Was at battle of Sheriffmuir; escaped from Arbroath on the same vessel with Lord Panmure, on whom he was in close attendance from the time of his rescue, and arrived with him at Avignon on 2 April 1716.

Black, William, Regent and Sub-Principal, King's College, Aberdeen

Sometimes described as "of Haddo." His daughter, Elizabeth, married Peter Farquharson of Inverey.

Blair, Dr Robert, Physician to Lord Panmure

At the Battle of Sheriffmuir, escaped from Arbroath on the same vessel with Lord Panmure.

Blair, The Rev William, Church of Scotland Minister

Son of Rev Robert Blair, Minister of Alvah. Minister at Forglen in 1667, transferred to Fordyce in 1675. He married and had two sons and three daughters. He died in 1716.

Bowman, James, farmer, Aberdeenshire

Captured by the Dutch near Burntisland 11 January 1716.

Brebner, James, Merchant in Aberdeen

Succeeded his father, John Brebner in Cottown, as "heir in Over Corskie in the parish of Kinerney, 9 January 1709."

Brockie, James, Shipmaster, Aberdeen

Met at Mistress Hepburn's house on 22 September (see William Hepburn).

Brodie, George, Servant to Sir James Gordon of Park.

Brown, Andrew, Merchant, Fraserburgh

A warrant had been issued for his arrest, but he was allowed bail on promising he would "carrie himself Loyally to his Majesty King George."

Buchan, Major-General Thomas

Third son of James Buchan of Auchmacoy, who died in 1659, and his wife, Margaret, daughter of Alexander Seton of Pitmedden. Born about 1641.

Buchan, Major James, of Auchmacoy

Nephew of General Thomas Buchan, who had two brothers. Of these, the elder, Alexander, married Mary Ramsay and died leaving an only daughter, when Acuhmacoy passed to the next brother, James. He married Jean Fraser of Tyrie and had two sons, Alexander, a priest who died in 1716 and James, the Major above, the Laird. Married in 1707, Mary, second daughter of Sir John Forbes of Craigievar and widow of John Ramsay of Laithers. By her he had seven sons (Thomas, his heir being born in 1708) and died in 1726.

Burnes, Robert, *grandfather of Robert Burns*

The family originally was called Burnes; it was only because it was pronounced in Ayrshire as if written "Burns" that the Poet and his brother, about 1786, consulted together and agreed to drop Burnes and assume Burns.

Burnett, Andrew, of Eldrick

Second son of Robert Burnett of Elrick, Newmachar, by his first wife, Bessie, daughter of Andrew Burnett of Durris. Married Marjorie in 1707, elder daughter of Sir John Johnston, 4th Baronet of Caskieben, and by her had four sons and four daughters. Died in 1720, aged about 35, and his widow in October 1723.

Burnett, The Rev Andrew, Church of Scotland Minister in Aberdeen

Son of James Burnett, Burgess of Aberdeen. Described by Woodrow as "a very weak, empty volatile man, of no great parts of learning and just made a tool of to disturb the established constitution." He wrote *The Spiritual Anatomy of Man,* published in London, 1693. He married twice (1) Margaret, third daughter of Sir Alexander Burnett of Leys, widow of Alexander Burnett of Monboddo, and had at least five children by her; (2) Elizabeth Reid, widow of Adam Maltman, Merchant, Aberdeen. He died 24 Oct 1716.

Burnett, George, Apothecary

Met at Mistress Hepburn's house on 22 September (see William Hepburn).

Burnett, James, of Monboddo

Only son of Alexander, second of Monboddo, and his wife Margaret, daughter of Sir Alexander Burnett of Leys, 2nd Baronet. Born in 1688, married 3 Nov 1709 Elizabeth, daughter of Sir William Forbes of Craigievar. They had three daughters and eleven sons, amongst whom was the famour Lord Monboddo.

Burnett, John, Merchant, Aberdeen

Nicknamed "Bonnie John," he was son of John Burnett of "Daladies," descended from the family of Leys, and his wife, Agnes, daughter of Turnbull of Strathcathro. He married firstly, 15 June 1703, Katherine, second daughter of George Paton of Grandhome; their eldest son John, born 1704, also a merchant in Aberdeen, married Thoeodosia Stuart of Dens and from them are descended the Burnett-Stuarts of Dens and Crichie; secondly, Katherine, third daughter of John Gordon of Fechil, and had a son by her, James Burnett, Merchant in Aberdeen. He survived the Rising.

Burnett, Robert, junior, Merchant, Aberdeen 1715

Cornet in the Town's troop of thirty Horse.

Burnett, Thomas, of Kirkhill 1715

Son of Alexander Burnett, 1st of Kirkhill, Dyce. Married with two sons, Thomas and David, and a daughter Agnes. Died in Nov 1763.

Calder, Alexander, younger, of Aswanley (Glass) 1715

Merchant and coppersmith in Old Aberdeen. Married Katherine Forbes of Balfluig and died on 6 Feb 1768, aged 86.

Campbell, The Rev George, Church of Scotland Minister of Alvah

A native of Aberdeenshire, he received his degree at King's College in July 1672. He married on 20 January 1717, Elizabeth Barclay and had two sons, George and Archibald, and a daughter, Elizabeth. He died in Boyndie.

Cargill, Thomas, Auchtydonald 1715

Reputed to have been a poet. Married to Anna Abercromby.

Carnegie, John, Dyer, Aberdeen 1715

In St Nicholas Churchyard is a tombstone to: "John Carnegie, Litster in Aberdeen, who dyed 15th April 1735, aged 69, also Elizabeth Carnegie his spouse, who dyed 6th October 1726, aged 55, with James Carnegie, Litster in Abdn. their son, who dyed 22nd February 1744, aged 38, and Mary Thomson his spouse who dyed 7 Sept. 1768, aged 60". He was son of James Carnegie, Litster in Aberdeen, who died in 1705, and Jean Ferguson his wife.

Cattanach, George

Met at Mistress Hepburn's house on 22 September (see William Hepburn).

Cattanach, James, Baillie, Aberdeen

One of those who elected the new Jacobite Magistrates of Aberdeen, in the New Church on 29 September 1715.

Cattanach, John, of Bellastraid 1715 & 1745

Sometimes called George. Possibly a Mackintosh by descent. Married first a daughter of Robert Lumsden of Corrachree and secondly Jean Forbes of Belnabodach.

Cattanach, Patrick, in Mickle Mill, Ellon
Prevented Mr James Burnett, who had been Minister at the Presbytery of Ellon, from officiating in his own church on 16 October 1715.

Catto, James, Shipmaster, Fraserburgh
In May 1716 a warrant had been issued for his arrest, but was allowed bail on promising he would "carrie himself Loyally to his Majesty King George under penalty of 500 merks Scots." Perhaps the father of William Catto, Merchant in Aberdeen, at Marischal College in 1719.

Chalmers, Charles, Portlethan
Second son of James Chalmers, Prof of Philosophy at Marischal College. Maried first Jean, daughter of Alexander Boog of Burnhouses, Berwickshire and then Helen, daughter of Alexander Young, Bishop of Liverpool. Was killed at Sheriffmuir, 13 Nov 1715.

Chalmers, The Rev George, Church of Scotland Minister of Botriphnie
Married in 1585, Margaret, daughter of Henry Stewart of Newton of Boharm, and had two sons. He died on 24 Feb 1727 in his 73rd year.

Chalmers, Dr Patrick, Professor of Medicine, Marischal College, Aberdeen
Eldest son of Rev William Chalmers, Minister of Skene. Died about 1727.

Charles, Alexander, Procurator, Aberdeen
Born in 1672. Married 2 Dec 1701, Margaret, only child of James Liddell, mathematic tutor at Marischal College, and by her had four sons and two daughters. Died on 25 March 1754, aged 82.

Clark, Captain, Portsoy
Menioned in Major Fraser's MS.

Clark, Alexander, Shipmaster in Portsoy

Clark, Alexander, Shipmaster, Banff
Born between 1670-1680, was a shipowner in Banff and traded between there and Holland. Before 1709 he married Christian Gordon, and had ten children. Died 8 Oct 1732.

Clark, John, Merchant, Aberdeen
Son of John Clark, merchant in Aberdeen. Married in 1710, Anna, daughter of Walter Cochran of Drumbreck (Provost of Aberdeen 1691-2) and his wife Margaret Butler. Died before 1736.

Collison, Charles, of Auchlunies
Son of Thomas Collison of Auchlunies and his wife, Jean Menzies, and grandson of John Collison, Provost of Aberdeen in 1594. Died in 1749 when the financial affairs of the family were at a low ebb.

Cook, Thomas, farmer, Aberdeenshire
Captured by the Dutch near Burntisland 11 January 1716

Cook, Thomas
Tenant of David Lumsden of Cushnie "forced to be in the Rebellion by the threats and force of the Earl of Mar" and taken prisoner at Preston in November 1715 with 12 other tenants of David Lumsden or Harry Lumsden of Auchindoir and Robert Reid of Mid Clove. Transported from Liverpool to Virginia in 1716.

Cooper, Alexander, Music-Master, Aberdeen

Married in 1705 Margaret, daughter of Alexander Robertson, Town Clerk of Aberdeen, and his first wife Barbara Cruickshank. Children named Alexander, John, George, Anna, Issobell and Christian. Died in 1722.

Cow, John

Reference in the Jacobite Cess Roll for Aberdeenshire in 1715 "1st February 1716 John Cow was paid £10".

Crichton, James, of Auchingoul

Son of George Crichton of Auchingoul (younger brother of James, 1st Viscount Frendraught) who married, before 1665, Jean, daughter of Sir Alexander Irvine of Drum. He died before 16 November 1744 having apparently disinherited the eldest of his four sons.

Cruickshank, George, Merchant and Baillie, Aberdeen

Son of George Cruickshank of Berriehillock, Dean of Guild in Aberdeen, 1664. "George Cruickshank younger, merchant, late Masater of the Kirk-work, and Anna Gordon, his spouse, had a son named Alexander, baptized 9 Jan 1698." Died in 1737.

Cruickshank, George

Jacobite at Fraserburgh where the town was searched for the arms left by Lord Lovat and John Forbes of Culloden. These were delivered to George Keith, younger of Ludquharn.

Cumine, George, of Pitullie

Born in 1695, he was the only son, by his third marriage, of William Cuming of Lochtervandick, Provost of Elgin, who sold Lochtervandich to Alexander Duff of Braco, and bought Auchry and Pitullie. Married in 1719 Jean, daughter of Capt Robert Urquhart of Burdsyards, by whom he had four sons and two daughters. Jean Urquhart died in 1728, and in 1731 he married his cousin, Christian, daughter of Sir John Guthrie of Ludquharn, and had by her seventeen children! He died on 12 December 1767 at Pittendrum, aged 72.

Cumming, John, Merchant, Aberdeen

Taxer appointed by the Town of Aberdeen.

Dalgarno, Mr James, Chamberlain to the Earl Marischal

Jacobite at Fraserburgh where the town was searched for the arms left by Lord Lovat and John Forbes of Culloden. These were delivered to George Keith, younger of Ludquharn. Son of Rev William Dalgarno and his wife Anna Keith.

Davidson, Alexander, of Newton

Eldest son of Alexander Davidson, and his first wife, Jean Burnett. Married on 2 Nov 1701 at Fyvie Church, Mary Gordon of Gight. He had seven children, and Alexander, the son who succeeded took the name of Gordon. He died in 1732.

Davidson, James, of Tillymorgan

Second son of Alexander Davidson of Newton. Died on 17 September 1720, unmarried, his nephew Alexander Davidson Gordon of Gight was served heir in 1735.

Davidson, Patrick, Ground Officer at Aboyne

Tenant of the Earl of Aboyne.

Davidson, William

Tenant of David Lumsden of Cushnie "forced to be in the Rebellion by the threats and force of the Earl of Mar" and taken prisoner at Preston in November 1715 with 12 other tenants of David Lumsden or Harry Lumsden of Auchindoir and Robert Reid of Mid Clove. Transported from Liverpool to Virginia on the *Friendship* 24 May 1716, landed in Maryland August 1716.

Day, John, Porter, King's College, Aberdeen

Was suspected of being a sympathiser.

Deuchar, Alexander, Merchant, Aberdeen

Donald, James, Banchory-Ternan

Donaldson, John, Writer in Turriff and Banff

Douglas, Rev George, Catholic Priest (also known as Dalgleish)

Son of Colin Douglas and his wife Elizabeth Irvine, born in 1681. He went to the Scots College in Rome in 1698 and returned to Scotland in April 1706. Thought to have been ordained in 1707 in the Highlands by Bishop Gordon, which, if it is true, was the first ordination in the country since the Reformation. He died in Morar on 29 April 1748.

Douglas, John, Marchant, Aberdeen

Son of Sylvester Douglas of Whiteriggs

Douglas, Patrick

Nephew of Sylvester Douglas of Whiteriggs

Douglas, The Rev Robert, Minister of Bothwell

Younger son of the Rev Robert Douglas, Bishop of Dunblane, brother to Sylvester Douglas of Whiteriggs.

Douglas, Sylvester, of Whiteriggs

Eldest son of Robert Douglas, Bishop of Dunblane. Married Margaret, daughter of Major George Keith of Whiteriggs, and thus obtained the estate in 1703.

Douglas, William

Nephew of Sylvester Douglas of Whiteriggs.

Duff, Alexander, of Drummuir

First cousin of William Duff, eldest son of Provost William Duff of Inverness and his first wife, Christian, daughter of Alexander Duff of Kinloss. Born in 1657 and married in 1684, Katherine, orphan daughter of Adam Duff, bankrupt Laird of Drummuir. By her he had eleven children, amongst them a daughter Anne, born 1684, who married Lachlan Mackintosh. Died in 1726.

Duff, John, Messenger, Aberdeen

Son of John Duff of Aberdeen of the Muldavit family and his wife Margaret Johnstone. Reported to have died in Rotterdam in 1718, but also that he was drowned returning with Taylor of Boyndie in 1718 and both their bodies got clasped with a rope and an oak plank. "Boyndie, in life, got on the shore of Musselburgh, retained the black mark of the log on his head, but Duff drowned."

Duff, William, of Dipple

Uncle of successor of William Duff of Braco, was second son of Alexander Duff of Keithmore and Helen Grant of Allachie. He married twice, first, Jean Gordon of Edinglassie, and secondly, Jean Dunbar of Durn. By his first wife he was the father of William, Lord Braco, afterwards first Lord Fife. He had three other sons who died young, and ten daughters, of whom the eldest, Helen, married the Hon William Sutherland. Two younger daughters were named Anne and Janet.

Duff, William, of Inverness
Father of Alexander Duff of Drummuir, and third son of Adam Duff of Clunybeg. Born in 1632. Died before end 1715.

Duguid, Alexander, Auchinhove, brother of Robert Duguid
Lieutenant under Glenbucket's command. Nephew to Dr Patrick Abercromby.

Duguid, Patrick Leslie, younger of Auchinhove 1715 & 1745
Son of Robert Duguid of Auchinhove, born in 1700, educated abroad and returned from Douai just before Rising of 1715. He married in 1730 Isabella Dickson, by whom he had three sons and one daughter, all dying in infancy. He married secondly, in 1740, Amelia, daughter of John Irvine of Kingcausie, by whom he had eleven children, the fourth son, John, ultimately succeeding him. Patrick Leslie Duguid's second wife having died in 1762, he married for the third time, in 1773, his cousin Eliza, sister of Patrick Leslie Grant. Died at the house of Tullos on 11 April 1777.

Duguid, Robert, of Auchinhove
9th Laird of Auchinhove and eldest son of Francis Duguid, 8th of Auchinhove and his wife, Marie Abercromby. Francis died in 1698 and in 1699 Robert married Teresa Leslie, third daughter of Patrick, Count Leslie of Balquhain. By her he had a family of four sons, the eldest being Patrick Leslie Duguid, his heir, and two daughters. Died in 1731.

Duguid, Patrick Leslie, younger of Auchinhove

Dunbar, Sir James, of Durn
Eldest son of Sir William Dunbar, 1st Baronet of Durn, and his wife Janet, daughter of John Brodie, Dean of Auldearn. Baptized on 9 January 1665; he married in 1692, Mary (or Margaret) daughter of James Baird, younger of Auchmedden, and by her had two sons, William, who succeeded him and James of Kincorth. Died in November 1737, his wife having predeceased him in 1734.

Dunbar, Jerome
Tenant of David Lumsden of Cushnie "forced to be in the Rebellion by the threats and force of the Earl of Mar" and taken prisoner at Preston in November 1715 with 12 other tenants of David Lumsden or Harry Lumsden of Auchindoir and Robert Reid of Mid Clove. Some were transported to Virginia. Jerome Dunbar returned from there.

Dunbar, The Rev William, Church of Scotland Minister of Cruden
Made Bishop in 1727 and in 1731 was recognised as Bishop of Moray and Ross. He died in 1746, aged 85.

Dunbreck (or Dumbreck), The Rev Patrick, Episcopalian Clergyman
Dunn (or Deune), attending Aberdeen University classes in 1680.

Dunn, James, Merchant in Aberdeen

Erroll, Charles, 13th Earl of

Eldest son of Sir John Hay, 12th Earl of Erroll, and Lady Anne Drummond, only daughter of James, 3rd Earl of Perth. Between 1712-15 lived on the Continent. Died, unmarried, 16 October 1717 aged 40, when the title devolved on his elder sister, Mary, Countess of Erroll. He had another sister Margaret.

Erskine, James

Uncle to the Laird of Pittodrie. Younger son of Thomas Erskine of Pittodrie who in 1643 married Helen, daughter of Sir William Auchinleck of Balmanno. Married a Mowat "heiress of Balquholly".

Erskine, Thomas, of Pittodrie

Eldest son of William Erskine, 6th of Pittodrie and his wife Mary, daughter of Patrick Grant of Ballindalloch. Married twice, in 1705 to Margaret, daughter of Sir Alexander Burnett of Craigmyle, by whom he had a son William, who, being weak in mind, was excluded from the succession to Pittodrie, and secondly on 30 November 1746 the Hon Anne Forbes, daughter of James, 16th Lord Forbes. By her he had an only daughter, Mary, his successor. Died on 14 October 1761 "at a very advanced age" Anne Forbes died at Pittodrie in November 1750, aged only twenty-seven.

Erskine, William

Brother to Thomas Erskine of Pittodrie. Died in Feb 1774, aged 86.

Ewan, George

Brother of John Ewan, tenant of the Earl of Aboyne.

Ewan, John

Tenant of the Earl of Aboyne.

Ewan, William, in Greencoats

Son of John Ewan, tenant of the Earl of Aboyne.

Farquharson, Alexander (or Alistair), younger of Auchindryne

Eldest son of Lewis Auchindryne. Married in 1721 Claudia, youngest daughter of Charles Innes of Drumgask. Had two sons and two daughters, the elder son Alexander succeeding to Auchindryne and Inverey.

Farquharson, Charles, Inverey

Second son of John Farquharson. Writer to the Signet in 1708. Died, unmarried, in 1747, succeeded by his half-brother James of Balmoral.

Farquharson, Charles, of Balmoral

Eldest son of William Farquharson of Inverey and his second wife, Agnes (or Anna), daughter of Alexander Gordon of Abergeldie. Half-brother to John Farquharson. Died unmarried before November 1718.

Farquharson, Charles, Whitehouse

Second son of Harry Farquharson of Whitehouse. Married daughter of Grant of Garthenmore and had two daughters.

Farquharson, Daniel, Merchant in Aberdeen

Taxer appointed by the Town of Aberdeen.

Farquharson, Donald, of Micras

Younger of two sons of Alexander Farquharson, 3rd of Allanquoich by Jean Forbes of Skellater. Maried firstly Murrel Gordon, daughter of Tirriesoul and secondly in 1726 Jean, daughter of James Grant of Gellovie and Knockando.

Farquharson, Donald, of Coldrach

Eldest son of George Farquharson of Coldrach and his wife, Margaret Farquharson, daughter of Allanquoich. Alive still in 1733. By his first wife, Grizel Small of Diranean, he had two sons, George and William.

Farquharson, Francis, younger of Whitehouse

Eldest son of Harry Farquharson of Whitehouse and his first wife Barbara Ross of Auchlossan. Married his cousin, Euphemia Ross of Auchlossan, and died in 1733.

Farquharson, George, younger of Coldrach

Son of Donald Farquharson of Coldrach and his first wife Grizel Small. Married Marjory (or Mary), duaghter of John Farquharson of Inverey and had five children, but only two sons, James and Donald and one daughter were alive in 1733. George died before that year. The elder son, James, who was served heir to his grandfather Donald, in 1751 married Mary Lumsden.

Farquharson, Harry, of Whitehouse

The third Farquharson Laird, he was the only son by the second marriage of James Farquharson WS. He married Barbara Ross of Auchlossan and had Francis and two other children. He married secondly, Elspet Harper, who had been his servant, and by her had Harry of Whitehouse-Mill, who was killed at Culloden.

Farquharson, Harry, of Cults

Son of Arthur Farquharson of Cults (Glengairn).

Farquharson, James, of Balmoral

Half-brother to the Charles and Peter Farquharson. Youngest son by the second marriage of John Farquharson of Inverey and his wife Marjory, daughter of George Leith of Overhall. Married Jane, daughter of William Leith of the Overhall family, but had no children. Merchant in Aberdeen. Died about 1753.

Farquharson, John, of Kirkton of Aboyne

Son of Thomas, son of John, third son of Finlay Farquharson, who was second son of Robert Farquharson, 1st of Invercauld. Married twice, first to Helen, daughter of Dr William Muir, Archdeacon of St Andrews and secondly to a daughter of Dr Alexander Pennycuick of Newhall of Ramanno.

Farquharson, John, Auchindryne

Second son of Lewis Farquharson. Born 15 April 1699. Died 22 August 1782 at Balmoral.

Farquharson, John, Whitehouse

Third and youngest son of Harry Farquharson of Whitehouse. Married and had three daughters. Described as "a surgeon in London".

Farquharson, Lawrence, in Cobletown of Tullich

Son of Donald Farquharson in Cobletown of Tullich, eldest son of Donald Farquharson, 2nd of Allanquoich by his second wife, Helen Garden. Transported from Liverpool to the West Indies, where he lived and died.

Farquharson, Lewis, of Auchindryne

Eldest son of James Farquharson, 1st of Inverey, and his second wife, Agnes Ferris. Entered a contract of marriage on 18 December 1693, with his cousin Margaret, second daughter of Alexander Farquharson of Allanaquoich, by whom he had six sons, Alexander, John, William, Donald, Charles and James. He also had three daughters. Died before 30 Nov 1729.

Farquharson, Peter, of Inverey

Eldest son of John Farquharson, 3rd of Inverey and his first wife, Margaret Gordon. Peter, sometimes called Patrick, married twice, first to Margaret, daughter of Thomas Nairn, Kirkhill, Perthshire by whom he had three daughters, and secondly to Elizabeth, daughter of William Black, Sub-Principal of King's College, Aberdeen, by whom he had three sons and two daughters. Died in 1737, succeeded by his son Joseph, afterwards by his son Benjamin. His widow survived him till 1766.

Farquharson, Peter, of the Whitehouse family

Grandson of James Farquharson, 1st of Whitehouse. Died in 1715 after an unsuccessful leg amputation.

Farquharson, Robert, of Allanquoich

Uncle of Lawrence in Cobletown of Tullich. Second son of Donald, 2nd of Allanquoich, and Helen Garden, daughter of Bellamore. Married Mary, daughter of Peter Gordon of Minmore, but left only a natural son.

Farquharson, Shaw, of the Achriachan family

Sixth son of Gregor Farquharson of Wester Camdell, who married Mary, daughter of John Mackenzie of Dalmore. Shaw was killed at Sheriffmuir.

Farquharson, Thomas, Merchant, Aberdeen

Taxer appointed by the Town of Aberdeen.

Ferguson, Francis

Tenant of David Lumsden of Cushnie "forced to be in the Rebellion by the threats and force of the Earl of Mar" and taken prisoner at Preston in November 1715 with 12 other tenants of David Lumsden or Harry Lumsden of Auchindoir and Robert Reid of Mid Clove. Transported from Liverpool to Antigua on the *Scipio* on 30 Mar 1716.

Ferries, George, farmer in Strathdon

Captured by the Dutch near Burntisland 11 January 1716.

Findlater, George, Excise Officer, Peterhead

Helped to break open the Clerk's room in Fraserburgh "with ane bigg hammer" and removed the "24 firelocks charged with powder and balls."

Findlater, John, Master of the Grammar School, Aberdeen

Son of Alexander Findlater, burgess of Aberdeen, born 1652. Died on 16 November 1717 aged 75, buried in St Nicholas Churchyard with his "beloved wives" Christian Burnet and Elizabeth Donaldson, and four children.

Finnie, John

Tenant of David Lumsden of Cushnie "forced to be in the Rebellion by the threats and force of the Earl of Mar" and taken prisoner at Preston in November 1715 with 12 other tenants of David Lumsden or Harry Lumsden of Auchindoir and Robert Reid of Mid Clove. Transported from Liverpool to Virginia 1716.

Fraser, Patrick, Catholic Priest

Forbes, Alexander, "youngest," Merchant in Aberdeen

Taxer appointed by the Town of Aberdeen.

Forbes, Alexander, younger of Balfluig

A younger son of John Forbes of Balfluig. Baptized on 8 May 1699.

Forbes, Alexander, Lord Pisligo

Born 1678. Escaped to Italy. Died 1762.

Forbes, Alexander, of Lockermick, Merchant, Aberdeen

The son of William Forbes in Lockermick, born in 1673. Married Janet Gordon and had at least one son, George. He died on 24 April 1738. His widow survived him.

Forbes, Alexander

Jacobite at Fraserburgh where the town was searched for the arms left by Lord Lovat and John Forbes of Culloden. These were delivered to George Keith, younger of Ludquham.

Forbes, The Hon Archibald

Born on 3 November 1697, third son of William, 13th Lord Forbes and his wife Anne, daughter of James Brodie of Brodie.

Forbes, Arthur, Echt, Merchant, Aberdeen

Taxer appointed by the Town of Aberdeen. At Marischal College, Aberdeen, from 1700 to 1704.

Forbes, Charles, Brux

Sixth son of Arthur Forbes, 10th of Brux and his wife Elizabeth Murray. Married and had a son, Captain Roderick, whoo died in Persia in 1760.

Forbes, Charles, Merchant, Aberdeen

Possibly younger brother of John Forbes of Upper Boyndlie, the Collector of Cess.

Forbes, George, of Culquhanny

Fourth son of Arthur Forbes of Culquhanny, born in 1687. Married 11 June 1708 to Elizabeth Gordon of Acuhindoir. His widow remarried in 1720.

Forbes, George, 4th of Skellater

Eldest son of George Forbes, 3rd of Skellater. Married twice, first in 1714 to Christian, daughter of John Forbes of Invererman and secondly, Isobel, daughgter of John Gordon of Blelack. He died in 1730 and was succeeded by his son, George.

Forbes, The Hon James

Second son of William, 13th Lord Forbes. He was born in 1689 and married twice, first in 1715 to Mary, daughter of Alexander, 3rd Lord Forbes of Pitsligo and widow of John Forbes, younger of Monymusk, by whom he had one son, James, and three daughters, and secondly, in August 1741, Elizabeth, daughter of Sir James Gordon, Bart. of Park, Banffshire, by whom he had no issue. He died in 1761.

Forbes, John, of Inverernan

The famous "Black Jock", he was born in 1666 or 1664, and married in 1684. Fifth son of William Forbes, 2nd of Skellater and only son of his second wife, Agnes, daughter of William McIntosh of Kyllachy and widow of Alexander McGillivray, younger of Drumnaglass. He married twice, first in 1684 to Elspet Stewart, by whom he had nine sons, and two daughters. His second wife, whom he married in 1709 was Margaret, daughter of the Rev Thomas Alexander, Minister of Logie Coldstone and had two sons by her. He died of wounds in 1716, a prisoner in Carlisle, a day before he was due to be hanged.

Forbes, John, of Belnabodach

Son of William Forbes and his wife Mary Stewart of Lesmurdie. He married on 7 November 1706, Janet, daughter of John Robertson, Minister of Invernochty.

Forbes, John, of Invernettie

Son of William Forbes of Ledinglassie, sometimes called "of Invernettie," who was brother of George, 3rd of Skellater. Married Rebecca (sometimes called Rachel) youngest daughter of John Forbes of Ledmacoy, and had at least one son, William. Shot in 1715 or 1716 by some dragoons commanded by Lord Forbes.

Forbes, John, of Upper Boyndlie

Fourth son of Sir John Forbes, 3rd of Monymusk, and his second wife Barbara, daughter of Sir John Dalmahoy, Bart. Born at Monymusk in 1680, he married on 27 April 1704 Susanna (born 1680) second daughter of George Morison of Bognie and Frendraught and had five sons and six daughters. Drowned November 1716.

Forbes, John, younger of Waterton

Eldest son of Thomas Forbes of Waterton and his first wife, Elizabeth Nicolson, second daughter of Sir George Nicholson of Balcaskie. Killed at Sheriffmuir.

Forbes, Lachlan, of Edinglassie

Fourth son of George Forbes, 3rd of Skellater, born in 1677. He married Margaret, daughter of Robert Irvine, Minister of Towie. He had at least one son, Benjamin.

Forbes, Nathaniel, of Ardgeith

Second son of George Forbes, 3rd of Skellater. Married with many children.

Forbes, Thomas, of Tolquhon family

Second son of Thomas Forbes of Little Auchry and his wife Henrietta, daughter of James Erskine, Lord Auchterhouse, he was born in 1689.

Forbes, Thomas

Tenant of David Lumsden of Cushnie "forced to be in the Rebellion by the threats and force of the Earl of Mar" and taken prisoner at Preston in November 1715 with 12 other tenants of David Lumsden or Harry Lumsden of Auchindoir and Robert Reid of Mid Clove. Transported from Liverpool to Virginia on the *Friendship* 24 May 1716, landed in Maryland Aug 1716, returned to Scotland 1722.

Forbes, Thomas of Tolquhon

Born 1689 son of Thomas Forbes of Little Auchry and Henrietta Erskine. Fled via London to France Sept 1716, died London 1728.

Forbes, William of Ellon

Forbes, William, of Blackton

Born 28 Nov 1699, son of Alexander Forbes of Blackton (King Edward) and his wife, Isobel Hacket, widow of Alexander Abernethy of Mayen. Born on 28 November 1689, he married twice, first on 31 Aug 1714 to Janet, sister of Joseph Brodie of Muiresk and had one daughter Isabel; secondly in 1722 Ann, daughter of Thomas Forbes of Gavell, by whom he had one son who died before his father. Died on 9 Oct 1771.

Forbes, William, younger of Invernettie

Son of John Forbes, 3rd of Invernettie and his wife Rebecca Forbes of Ledmacoy. Born in 1694.

Forbes, William, of Tombeg

Son of John Forbes (of the Monymusk family) and Anna Lunan, daughter of the Minister of Monymusk. Born in 1687, he married Anna, daughter of Alexander Forbes, Minister of Fintray.

Forbes, William, Echt, Merchant, Aberdeen

Taxer appointed by the Town of Aberdeen. At Marischal College, Aberdeen, from 1700 to 1704.

Fraser, Lord Charles, of Muchals

Fourth and last Lord Fraser, only son of Andrew, 3rd Lord Fraser and his first wife, Katherine, daughter of the 7th Lord Lovat, widow of Viscount Arbuthnot and before that of Sir John Sinclair of Dunbeath. Born in Sept 1662, in Sept 1683 he married Mary or Marjorie Erskine, daughter of James, 7th Earl of Buchan and widow of Simon Fraser of Inverallochy. He died by falling from a cliff at Pennan on 12 October 1716.

Fraser, The Hon James, of Lonmay

Third son of William, 11th Lord Saltoun and his wife Margaret, daughter of James Sharpe, Archbishop of St Andrews. Married in 1726 Lady Eleanor Lindsay,m daughter of Colin, 3rd Earl of Balcarres, and had one son, William, who died abroad. Died on 10 Aug 1729; his widow surviving him for six years.

Fraser, Captain Simon

Cousin to William Fraser of Inverallochy, he was son of a younger brother of the Simon of Inverallochy, who married Lady Marjorie Erskine.

Fraser, William, of Inverallochy

Stepsun of Lord Charles of Muchals. Second son of Simon Fraser of Inverallochy and his wife Lady Marjorie Erskine, daughter of the Earl of Buchan. Killed at Sheriffmuir.

Fullarton, James, Advocate, Aberdeen

Third son of Robert Udny of Auchterellon and Elizabeth, only daughter of Col John Fullarton of Dudwick, James assumed the name of Fullarton. Married Jean Walker and had six sons and five daughters. He is supposed to have died in 1761.

Fullarton, John, of Dudwick

Brother of James Fullarton, second son of Robert Udny of Auchterellon, he took the name of Fullarton when he succeeded his maternal grandfather in Dudwick in 1689. Married Mary, duaghter of Sir David Falconer of Newton, and had two sons and three daughters.

Fyfe, James, Baillie and Merchant, Aberdeen

Eldest son of John Fyfe, merchant in Aberdeen, and Elizabeth Tulloch his wife. He died 13 August 1729.

Garden, Charles, of Bellastrem

Garden, The Rev George, DD, Minister of St Nicholas Church, Aberdeen

Son of Rev Alexander Garden, Minister of Forgue, born in 1648. He escaped from captivity in Winton's House in the Canongate by changing clothes with his sister. He died 31 January 1733 in his 85th year, and was buried at Old Machar.

Garden, The Rev James, DD, Professor of Divinity in King's College, Aberdeen

Elder brother of Dr George Garden, born at Forgue in 1646, he graduated at Aberdeen in 1662. In 1696 he was living in Aberdeen with his wife and nine children. He died in 1726, aged about 80.

Gatt, The Rev James, Minister of Gretna

A native of Cullen, Banffshire, in 1714 he entered King's College, Aberdeen. Expelled for forcing the drummer of Old Aberdeen to make a proclamation in February 1716 desiring all persons to come and see the Duke of Brunswick burnt in effigy. He married Jean, daughter of the Rev James Gowanlock, Minister of Kikpatrick-Fleming, and died 31 Oct 1787, in his 88th year.

Gellie, James, Merchant, Aberdeen

Married 8 April 1714 Elizabeth, eldest daughter of Alexander Thomson, Advocate and had at least two sons and a daughter. Died before 1744.

Gellie, Patrick, Merchant, Aberdeen

Taxer appointed by the Town of Aberdeen. Son of Patrick Gellie, merchant and burgess of Aberdeen. Owned Balgarse in Foveran. He is believed to have died before 1743.

Gordon, Adam, of Balgowan

Second son of William Gordon of Balgowan, Keig, and his wife Isobel Leith.

Gordon, Alexander, Merchant, Aberdeen

Married to Isobel, daughter of James Gordon, Dean of Guild, in 1710, and had five children.

17

Gordon, Alexander, of Blelack

Second son of John Gordon of Blelack, succeeding to title. Married firstly to Barbara Stewart and secondly to Isobel Forbes, who was described as "a masculine character," and had two sons, John and Charles. He died in 1723.

Gordon, Alexander, of Cairnfeld

Son of Robert Gordon, 6th of Cairnfield. Later a merchant in Amsterdam.

Gordon, Alexander, Commissary Clerk Depute, Aberdeen

Second son of John Gordon, 2nd of Seaton and Elizabeth Irvine, his wife. Born in 1688, he married Marjory, daughter of James Milne of Blairton and had three sons and two daughters. He died in 1727.

Gordon, Alexander, in Comrie

Married Jane, and had a son and a daughter before 1696.

Gordon, Alexander, brother of Glenbucket

Son of John Gordon of Knockespock.

Gordon, Alexander, of Glengerack

Son of Charles Gordon of Glengerack and Margaret Duff, eldest daughter of Alexander Duff of Braco. Born in 1698, he married in 1721 at Inchdrewer Castle, Helen Lauder, daughter of Sir John Lauder, 2nd Baronet of Fountainhall and widow of George, 4th Lord Banff.

Gordon, Alexander, Scurdargue

Was at Sheriffmuir.

Gordon, Alexander

Tenant of David Lumsden of Cushnie "forced to be in the Rebellion by the threats and force of the Earl of Mar" and taken prisoner at Preston in November 1715 with 12 other tenants of David Lumsden or Harry Lumsden of Auchindoir and Robert Reid of Mid Clove. Transported from Liverpool to Virginia on the *Friendship* 24 May 1716, landed in Maryland Aug 1716.

Gordon, Dr Alexander, Catholic Priest

Captured with Francis Gordon of Craig at Dunfermline on 24 October 1716. Probably son of Patrick of Glastirem and uncle of James of Glastirem. Although too ill to march to Carlisle, he survived the rising and retired to Auchindour and died there at an advanced age in 1763.

Gordon, Charles, of Abergeldie

Son of Gordon of Minmore. Married Rachel, daughter of Alexander Gordon, 8th Laird and Euphemia Graham of Morphie. They had three sons, Peter, Alexander and Joseph.

Gordon, Charles, of Buthlaw, Advocate, Aberdeen

Son of William Gordon of Buthlaw and his wife Elizabeth, daughter of Captain Robert Martin of Clerkhill, near Peterhead. Married Jean, daughter of John Udny of Cultercullen and part of Newtyle and by her had six sons and seven daughters. He died 23 Dec 1751 at a very advanced age.

Facies Ciuitatis ABERDONIÆ Vet.

he Proſpect of Old ABERDIEN.

the plate in
Aulan 1693

Gordon, Charles, of Tilphoudie

Eldest son of John Gordon, 8th of Tilphoudie by his second wife Elizabeth Duguid of Auchinhove, said to have been killed at Sheriffmuir.

Gordon, Francis, of Craig, 7th Laird

Eldest son of Francis, 6th Laird of Craig, and his first wife, Elizabeth, daughter of Sir Gilbert Menzies of Pitfodels. Born about 1653, he died of wounds in September 1716 at Stirling. He had married Agnes Ogilvie, eldest daughter of George, 2nd Lord Banff and had three sons and five daughters. His second wife was Anna, daughter of William Gordon of Corrachree.

Gordon, Francis, younger of Craig

Eldest son of 7th Laird. Born about 1680 and died in 1727 in England. Married three times, firstly to Elizabeth Barclay of Towie, widow of John Gordon of Rothiemay - no issue; secondly Agnes Forbes of Balfluig, mother of John, 9th Laird of Criag; and thirdly Catherine Campbell of Lundie, widow of Patrick Russell of Moncoffer, with issue, Francis and William.

Gordon, George, of Buckie

Twice married, first about 1706 to Jean Burnett by whom he had a son, George and a daughter, Katherine; secondly in 1717 to Margaret, daughter of George Gordon of Glasterim, and had two sons and four daughters. He died in 1729.

Gordon, George, of Carnousie

Second son of Sir George Gordon of Edinglassie and his second wife, Jean Forbes. Married Jean, daughter of Arthur Forbes of Brux, and had four sons, including Arthur, younger of Carnousie, and four daughters.

Gordon, George, of Dorlaithers

Second son of Alexander Gordon of Auchintoul, Lord Auchintoul and his wife, Isobel Gray, daughter of Gray of Braik. He married Barbara, daughter of Alexander Mackenzie of Artloch, and by her had three sons, and one daughter. Perished at sea escaping to Holland.

Gordon, George, of Glastirem

Second son of Patrick Gordon of Glastirem, married Violet, daughter of Michael Strachan of Auchnagatt. He died in 1721.

Gordon, George, of Kincardine Mill

Son of John, and married to Agnes Gordon, he died before 1720.

Gordon, George, of Sauchen

Gordon, Harry, of Avochie

Eldest son of John Gordon of Avochie. His mother was Isobel Farquharson and his wife was Elizabeth, sister to John Gordon of Glenbucket. They had a son, John.

Gordon, James, of Barnes

Son of George, 1st of Shellagreen, he married Marjorie, one of the eight daughters of John Moir of Barnes and Mary Cochrane; the issue of the marriage being seven daughters but apparently no son. He died before 1739.

Gordon, James, of Ellon

Son of Alexander Gordon, farmer in Bourtie. He married Elizabeth Livingstone and had five sons and six daughters. He died in 27 Feb 1732.

Gordon, Dr James, of Hilton

Son of Dr John Gordon of Collieston. Married in 1731 Barbara, daughter of Robert Cuming of Birnes, by whom he had a son John. He died in 1755.

Gordon, James, of Letterfourie

Son of John Gordon of Letterfourie and his first wife, Janet Seton. Married in 1695, Glicerie, daughter of Sir James Dunbar, 2nd Baronet of Durn and had four sons and three daughters. He died in 1748, aged 88.

Gordon, James, younger of Auchlyne

Second son of James, 2nd of Auchlyne and his wife, Rachel Burnett, the younger James is also called "of Tillyfour". He married Ann, second daughter of James Sandilands and had one son, James, another son and three daughters. Killed in 1715, presumably at Sheriffmuir.

Gordon, James, Brewer, Aberdeen

Caputred at Dunfermline 24 Oct 1715 and marched to Edinburgh and then Carlisle 4 Sep 1716 where he was discharged.

Gordon, James, Dean of Guild, Aberdeen

Married to Janet Paton, had a son, George, baptized on 21 Jul 1706, and on 27 April 1710 had a daughter, Isobel. He was buried on 31 Jan 1728, and Jean Strachan, spouse was buried with him on 5 Mar 1728.

Gordon, James, of Balgowan

Son of Adam, of Balgowan.

Gordon, James, of Park

Son of Sir John Gordon, 1st Baronet of Park and his fourth wife, Helen Ogilvy, daughter of James, 2nd Earl of Airlie. Married twice, firstly in 1709 to Helen Fraser, daughter of William, 11th Lord Saltoun and by her had William, John and Helen, and secondly about 1720, Margaret Elphinstone, daughter of John, 8th Lord Elphinstone and widow of George Leslie of Balquhain, who died in 1715. By this second marriage he had one son, James Gordon of Cobairdy and three daughters. Died 15 Dec 1727 of apoplexy.

Gordon, Rev James, Glastirem, Catholic Priest

Son of Patrick Gordon of Glastirem and brother of George Gordon of Glastirem, the family being cadets of Letterfourie. Born in 1664, was sent to the Scots College in Paris in 1680. He died in 1746 at Thornhill, near Drummond Castle.

Gordon, John, of Achanacy

A prisoner in Banff in November 1716.

Gordon, John, of Achindachy

Eldest son of Alexander Gordon, 3rd of Auchindachy, who died about 1713, and his wife Katherine Martin. In 1714 he married Jean, eldest daughter of George Innes of Dunkinty, Provost of Elgin, and they had a son, Alexander, and one daughter. There exists a testament of how he beat his wife, who on a number of occasions was only saved by the intervention of others. The House of Auchindachy was described as "ruinous" in 1742. Probably died in 1749. What became of his son is not known.

Gordon, John, of Coldstone
Buried at Lancaster between January and July 1716.

Gordon, Dr John, of Collieston
Son of another Dr John Gordon of Collieston and his first wife, Katherine Fullarton. Married Margaret Dowell and had nine sons, amongst whom was Dr James of Hilton, and several daughters. He died in 1735.

Gordon, John, Cromar
Son of a tenant in Cromar. He refused to serve and was taken prisoner by the Jacobites.

Gordon, John, of Dumeath
Son of Patrick Gordon of Dunmeath, Banff.

Gordon, John, younger of Lesmoir
Fourth son of Sir James Gordon, 4th Baronet of Lesmoir by his wife, Jane, only daughter of Sir John Gordon of Haddo. Later married Henrietta, daughter of 11th Lord Saltoun by whom he had four sons and six daughters.

Gordon, Dr John, of Seaton, Civilist, King's College
Eldest son of James Gordon, 1st of Seaton, Commissary Clerk, and Marjorie, daughter of Robert Forbes of Rubislaw. Married Elizabeth, only daughter of Richard Irvine of Cairnfield, and had two sons, Richard and Alexander and three daughters. Buried on 28 September 1741.

Gordon, The Rev Ludovick, Minister of Kinoir
Son of the Rev James Gordon, Minister of Rothiemay and his wife, Katharine, and became Laird of Kinmundy. Married to Anna Gordon, he had Alexander and Jean.

Gordon, Patrick, of Auchleuchries
Third son of John Gordon of Auchleuchries and his wife, Elizabeth, daughter of William Grant of Crichie.

Gordon, Patrick, Bogs, North Rhynie
Gordon, Patrick
Tenant of the Earl of Aboyne.

Gordon, Peter, in Drumbulg
Gordon, Richard, Regent of King's College, Aberdeen
Eldest son of John Gordon of Seaton, Civilist, Richard was born in 1687. Married first in 1730 Elizabeth, daughter of John Leith of Leith Hall, with two daughters and secondly, Mary Auchindachy, by whom he had one son, John, and two daughters. Died 9 November 1763, aged 77.

Gordon, Robert, of Cluny
Son of Robert Gordon of Cluny, Advocate. Married with a son, Robert, who served heir to him in Cluny in 1723.

21

Gordon, Robert, of Hallhead

Son of Patrick Gordon, 9th Laird of Hallhead. Successful wine merchant in Bordeaux. Married Isabel Byres of Tonley and his son was George of the '45. Died in 1738.

Gordon, Robert, younger of Lesmoir

Fifth son of Sir James Gordon.

Gordon, Robert, Scurdargue

Brother of Alexander Gordon of Scurdargue. Fought at Sheriffmuir. He married his own near relative, Elizabeth Gordon of Tolophin, and had children, among them Alexander (1724-1807).

Gordon, William, of Craigwillie

Gordon, William, of Goval

Second son of James Gordon, 1st of Seaton. Married Christian Wyllie and then, before 1710, Elizabeth, daughter of Robert Cruickshank of Banchory, widow of John Johnston, Provost of Aberdeen in 1697. Had sons William and Nathaniel. Died in 1733.

Gordon, William, Merchant, Kintore

May have been a relative of Captain James Gordon, son of Patrick, 1st of Badenscoth, because he witnessed the baptism of Isobel, his daughter, on 23 Oct 1702.

Gordon, William, 3rd of Farskane

Grandson of William, 1st of Farskane, and son of William, 2nd Laird and Helen, second daughter of Alexander Duff of Braco, married before 1700. Married Margaret, daughter of James Duff of Crombie in 1725. Probably died in Norway where he was a merchant.

Grant, Robert

Tenant of David Lumsden of Cushnie "forced to be in the Rebellion by the threats and force of the Earl of Mar" and taken prisoner at Preston in November 1715 with 12 other tenants of David Lumsden or Harry Lumsden of Auchindoir and Robert Reid of Mid Clove. Transported from Liverpool to Maryland on *Godspeed* on 28 Jul 1716, landed in Maryland Oct 1716.

Grant, William

Tenant of David Lumsden of Cushnie "forced to be in the Rebellion by the threats and force of the Earl of Mar" and taken prisoner at Preston in November 1715 with 12 other tenants of David Lumsden or Harry Lumsden of Auchindoir and Robert Reid of Mid Clove. Transported from Liverpool to Virginia on the *Friendship* 24 May 1716, landed in Maryland Aug 1716.

Gray, The Rev Alexander, Minister, Footdee

Son of Thomas Gray, Provost of Aberdeen, born about 1660. Burgess of Aberdeen 1695.

Gray, John, Baillie, Fraserburgh

A warrant had been issued for his arrest, but he was allowed bail on promising he would "carrie himself Loyally to his Majesty King George."

Gray, Patrick

Convenor of the Trades of Aberdeen, died 1736.

Gray, Patrick, Convener of the Trades, Aberdeen
Died before 13 Nov 1736.

Gray, William, farmer, Aberdeenshire
Captured by the Dutch near Burntisland 11 January 1716.

Gray, William
Tenant of David Lumsden of Cushnie "forced to be in the Rebellion by the threats and force of the Earl of Mar" and taken prisoner at Preston in November 1715 with 12 other tenants of David Lumsden or Harry Lumsden of Auchindoir and Robert Reid of Mid Clove. Some were transported to Virginia.

Halket, George
Schoolmaster at Rathen in 1714, deprived in 1723, died at Memsie 1756 and was buried in Fraserburgh. Married in March 1718, Janet Adamson, daughter of Marion Crawford in Rathen, and had three children.

Hamilton, John, Janitor, King's College, Aberdeen
Discharged from his post on 1 May 1716.

Hamilton, John, of Gibston (1715 and 1745)
Tenant of the Duke of Gordon. Married to Janet Mitchell. From Newgate he was hanged on Kennington Common on Nov 1746. He had a son, also named John who succeeded him as Factor to the Duke of Gordon.

Harper, The Rev Adam, Minister of Boharm
Eldest son of the Rev William Harper, Minister of Boharm, and his wife, Elizabeth, daughter of Walter Innes of Auchlunkart. He married twice: (1) 2 Oct 1687, Janet, daughter of Alexander Leslie of Kininvie, by whom he had four sons and three daughters; (2) 31 August 1703, Margaret, daughter of Alexander Gordon of Arradoul, and by her had three sons and six daughters. He died 14 May 1726, aged about 67.

Hay, Alexander, of Ambath
Son of Alexander Hay of Ambath, who was son of George Hay of Rannes and his wife, Agnes Guthrie, daughter of the Bishop of Moray.

Hay, Alexander, younger of Ambath
Was imprisoned and claimed to have been forced to join the Jacobite cause. After his release he went abroad and in his sixties was said to be a very rich man, probably by selling Spa water.

Hay, Alexander, conjunct Sheriff-Clerk, Aberdeen
One of the sons of Thomas Hay, Sheriff-Clerk and his wife, Jean King. Had brother called Colin.

Hay, Charles, of Rannes
Eldest son of James Hay of Rannes and his wife, Margaret Gordon of Glengerack. Born in 1688. In 1710 he married Helen, only child of Dr Andrew Fraser of Inverness, and by her had two sons, of whom the elder, Andrew, took part in the '45, and five daughters. Died in London in 1751.

Hay, John, of Muldavit
Son of William Hay of Muldavit and his wife, Helen Crichton, sister of James, Viscount Frendraught, whom he married in 1663. Married

Katherine, eldest daughter of James Hay of Rannes in 1697. Died in 1720.

Hay, John, Barber

Met at Mistress Hepburn's house on 22 September (see William Hepburn).

Hay, Walter, of Lickleyhead

Brother of the Laird of Arnbath, and uncle of young Alexander Hay. He was dead by 18 Dec 1725, when his son, Alexander, was served heir to him.

Hay, William, Messenger

Met at Mistress Hepburn's house on 22 September (see William Hepburn).

Hay, The Rev William, Minister of Rothiemay

Married twice, but the name of his first wife is unknown though he had two sons and two daughters by her. His second wife, whom he married on 7 May 1700 was Ann, daughter of William Grant of Crichie. He was described at one point as "a scandalous drunkard." He died in January 1718.

Henderson, Robert

Tenant of David Lumsden of Cushnie "forced to be in the Rebellion by the threats and force of the Earl of Mar" and taken prisoner at Preston in November 1715 with 12 other tenants of David Lumsden or Harry Lumsden of Auchindoir and Robert Reid of Mid Clove. Transported from Liverpool to Virginia on *Friendship* 24 May 1716, landed in Maryland Aug 1716.

Hepburn, The Rev Alexander, Episcopal Minister of St Fergus and Peterhead

A native of Buchan. He married Eliza Clark, who died in 1703, and had two sons and three daughters. He died in Peterhead in 1737, aged about 81, and left behind him in manuscript a decription of Buchan in 1721.

Hepburn, William, Vintner, Merchant

On 22 September, a mob first met in Mistress Hepburn's and then came to the counsel house and required the armes and amunitions belonging to the town with the Keys of the Block house, seeing they were not to regard the magistrates any longer as magistrates."

Horn, John, of Westhall

Son of Rev James Horn and his wife Isobella, daughter of John Leslie, 7th of Pitcapel. Maried first Anna, daughter of Robert, 2nd Viscount Arbuthnott on 20 Nov 1693, and had a daughter, Anna. His second wife was Anna Simpson.

Hunter, The Rev William, Minister of Banff

Born about 1662, the son of Robert Hunter, Provost of Ayr and Martha Musket of Craighead, Perthshire. He married twice: (1) 27 Dec 1699, Anne, daughter of John Guthrie of King Edward and widow of Patrick Grant of Dunlugas, by whom he had a son Alexander, and other Children: (2) in 1723, Mary Ogilvie, daughter of George, 3rd Lord Banff, and widow of John Joass of Colleonard. He died in 1730.

Idell, The Rev William, Minister of Coull

Born in Mar, he was schoolmaster of Chapel of Garioch in 1669.

Innes, Sir George, of Coxton

Son of Sir Alexander Innes, 1st Baronet of Coston and his first wife, Jean Rollo of Bannockburn. Married in 1706 Elizabeth, daughter of John Gordon of Rothiemay and his wife, Elizabeth Barclay, heiress of Towie. He had three sons, Alexander, John and James. Died at Scone in 1715, it is believed of wounds received at Sheriffmuir.

Innes, Colonel James 1715 & 1745

Third son of Sir Alexander Innes, 1st Baronet of Coston. Also involved in the '45 when almost 70 years old, and was executed on 21 Oct 1746 at Brampton. He left a wife, Mary Ramsay, and several daughters.

Innes, John, of Sinnahard

Son of John Innes of Towie, Culquoich and Sinnahard, he was the 4th Innes owner of Sinnahard and married in 1712 Anne Hay of Arnbath. Died 1725.

Innes, The Rev John, Minister of Gamrie

Was at King's College, Aberdeen in 1667. He married Margaret Gordon, who, with a daughter, survived him. He died on 14 June 1732, aged 82.

Innes, Father Lewis, Catholic Priest

Born in Walkerdale in the Enzie in 1651, was the second son of James Innes, 1st of Drumgask and his wife, Jane, daughter of Robert Robertson, Provost of Aberdeen. Sent to the Scots College in Paris, and in 1682 became its Principal. Confidential Secretary to Mary of Modena, Consort of King James VII. He died in Paris on 22 January 1738.

Irvine, Adam, of Brucklay 1715 & 1745

Son of the Rev Robert Irvine, Minister of Towie, and his second wife, Agnes, daughter of Patrick Murray of Blairfindy. Married in 1710, Margaret, daughter of Sir John Reid, 1st Baronet of Barra. He left two sons and two daughters.

Irvine, Alexander, younger of Drum

Son of Alexander Irvine of Murtle and his wife, Janet, daughter of Alexander Irvine of Drum. Died unmarried in 1735.

Irvine, James, Sheriff-Clerk of Kincardine

Son of Robert Irvine and Barbara Mitchell, his wife. Grandson of John Irvine "in Seattoun". He was married, with at least one son.

Irvine, John, of Kingcausie

Son of John Irvine of Kingcausie, who died in 1714 and his wife, Elizabeth, daughter of John Ramsay of Clush. Married Margaret, daughter of Thomas Forbes, merchant in Aberdeen by whom he had five sons and four daughters born between the years 1703 and 1723. His wife died on 30 December 1764 aged 83.

Irvine, John, Catholic Priest

Born in 1652, and in 1671 went to the Scots College in Rome. He left in 1679 and was for many years a missionary in Scotland, dying at Gordon Castle, 17 April 1717.

Irvine, William, of Artamford

Second son of James Irvine of Artamford and his wife, Margaret, daughter of James Sutherland of Kinminity, Keith.

Irvine, The Rev William, of Fortrie

Son of Alexander Irvine of Fortrie, parish of Ellon, he was born there about 1660. A strong Jacobite, he was present at Killiecrankie. He escaped from both Dundee and Fleet prisons, and lived subsequently in Linlithgow. He is described as being "of a forward and fiery temper, rough and blustering." He died in Edinburgh on 19 December 1725.

Jaffray, Andrew, of Ardtannies

Son of Provost Alexander Jaffray and his wife, Sarah Cant. A merchant in Aberdeen, he had a wife and ten children.

Jaffray, The Rev Andrew, Minister of Alford

Probably son of Alexander Jaffray, Minister of King Edward. Ordained deacon in 1674, he was deposed on 26 September 1716 for espousing the Jacobite cause. He married Marjory Davidson and had four sons.

Johnston, Sir John, of Caskieben

Son of John Johnston of New Place. His wife was Janet, daughter of Thomas Mitchell of Tilliegreig, Baillie of Aberdeen, and he had two daughters and an only son John, who predeceased him.

Johnston, John, younger of Caskieben

Only son of John Johnston born in 1690. Killed at Sheriffmuir.

Johnston, John, of Boginjoss

Second son of John Johnston of Bishopstown, Newhills, and his wife, Margaret Alexander. Married Christian Marnoch, by whom he had three sons and one daughter. He died in 1721.

Jollie, William

Jacobite at Fraserburgh where the town was searched for the arms left by Lord Lovat and John Forbes of Culloden. These were delivered to George Keith, younger of Ludquharn.

Keith, Alexander, of Northfield

Eldest son of George Keith of Northfield. Married Sophia, eldest daughter of John Fraser of Memsie, before 1693. Had at least two sons, Alexander and John, and one daughter, Anne.

Keith, George, Advocate, Aberdeen

Second son of Sir William Keith of Ludquharn. Died 24 Sept 1738.

Keith, The Rev James, Belhelvie

Keith, James

Born 16 Jun 1696 son of William Keith, Earl Marischal. Died Hochkirchen 14 Oct 1758.

Keith, John

Tenant of the Earl of Aboyne.

Keith, The Rev John, of Glasgowego

Keith, Sir William, of Ludquharn

Son and heir of Sir Alexander, 2nd Baronet of Ludquharn. Married a daughter of George Smith of Rapness and by her had two sons and one daughter, Mary. William, the elder son was from 1716 to 1726 Governor of Pennsylvania.

Kintore, William, 2nd Earl of
Eldest son of Sir John Keith. His wife Catharine was daughter of the 4th Viscount Stormont. His eldest son John, at 26 fought with his father at Sheriffmuir and was married to the daughter of Lord Grange (brother of the Earl of Mar whose wife was so mysteriously imprisoned on St Kilda). His younger son, William died without issue.

Law, The Rev Alexander, Minister of Kearn
Ordained Minister of Kearn on 31 March 1713 and deposed 4 April 1716.

Law, The Rev William, Minister of Slains
Appointed schoolmaster at Strichen in 1679. He was suspended from the ministry for erroneous doctrine.

Leith, Alexander, of Freefield
Second son of James Leith of New Leslie, afterwards of Leith Hall. He married Christian, daughter of Alexander Davidson of Newton, by whom he had four sons, Alexander, Walter, Patrick and George. He died on 4 April 1754, aged 90.

Leith, George, Secretary to Lord Erroll
Jacobite at Fraserburgh where the town was searched for the arms left by Lord Lovat and John Forbes of Culloden. These were delivered to George Keith, younger of Ludquham.

Leith, John, of Leith Hall
Eldest son of James Leith of New Leslie, Peil Syde, Arnbog, etc and Margaret Strachan of Glenkindie. Married Janet, daughter of George, 2nd Lord Banff and had five sons. Died in 1727.

Leith, The Rev Patrick, Minister of Lumphanan
Graduated at King's College, Aberdeen, 11 July 1676 and deposed on 4 September 1716 for engaging in the Rising.

Leslie, Charles "Mussel-Mou'd Charlie" 1715 & 1745
So called from a singular projection of his under-lip. He was born in 1667, a natural son of Leslie of Pitcaple. A ballad monger, described as a thin man, about 5 feet 10 inches in height, with small fiery eyes, a long chin and red hair. Died at Old Rayne in 1782 at the extraordinary age of 105 - probably the last survivor of the Rising of 1715.

Leslie, The Rev Charles, of Glasslough
The family of Leslie of Glasslough, Ireland is descended from the Wardes' branch of the family of Leslie of Balquhain. Born 17 July 1650 sixth son of Rev Charles Leslie, admitted to Trinity College, Dublin in 1664. He married Jane Leslie and had two sons, Robert and Henry.

Leslie, James, of the Warthilll family
Eldest son of Alexander Leslie, Minister of Crail in Fife, and his wife Helen, daughter of John Seymour, Minister of Macgill. Married Catherine Mills, and died in 1730, having had three sons and three daughters.

Leslie, John, Baillie, Aberdeen
Probably died around 18 September 1730.

Leslie, The Rev William, of Little Folla
Eldest son of George Leslie, 4th Laird of Little Folla and his wife, Isabella, daughter of William Cheyne of Kaithen. Sometime schoolmaster at Auchterless, he went to Ireland to assist his uncle in Fermanagh. He retired to Little Folla and died in 1722, aged 71.

Liddell, George, Professor of Mathematics, Marischal College, Aberdeen
Son of Duncan Liddell and his wife Jean Montgomery.

Lindsay, William, Goldsmith, Aberdeen
Taxer appointed by the Town of Aberdeen. Deacon-Convenor of the Incorporated Trades in 1713.

Lister, John, of Clerkseat
The son of Alexander Lister, Regent of Marischal College in 1682, John Lister was there from 1697 to 1701. Married Jean Gordon and had at least one son, Thomas.

Livingstone, The Rev Andrew, Minister of Keig
Married, he had three sons and one daughter, William, Andrew, Alexander and Margaret.

Livingstone, The Rev William, Minister of Deer
Ejected from the church in 1711, he took part in the 'Rabbling of Deer'. During the Rising of 1715 he "invaded" the church of Deer and prayed for the Old Chevalier and the success of his arms. He died in 1751.

Logan, John
Jacobite at Fraserburgh where the town was searched for the arms left by Lord Lovat and John Forbes of Culloden. These were delivered to George Keith, younger of Ludquharn.

Longmoor, William, Schoolmaster of Rothiemay

Lumsden, David, of Cushnie
Third son of Alexander Lumsden, 13th Laird of Cushnie and his second wife Elizabeth Leith of Whitehaugh. Born in 1682, he married Margaret, sister of Sir William Forbes of Craigievar, by whom he had one daughter, Margaret. He died on 23 December 1718.

Lumsden, Harry, younger of Auchindoir
Born in 1685, the eldest son of John Lumsden of Auchindoir and Corrachree, who married Agnes, daughter of Gordon of Auchlyne and Knockespock. Transported from Liverpool to Virginia on the *Friendship* 24 May 1716, landed Maryland Aug 1716, he returned to Scotland after two years. He married, firstly in 1720 Katherine, daughter of George Gordon of Buckie (she died in 1733) by whom he had at least two sons, John, Matthew and three daughters, and secondly, in 1736 Margaret, sister of Sir Archibald Foulis of Dunipace and widow of Peter Gordon of Ardmeallie, by whom there was no issue. Died in 8 June 1754, aged 69.

Lunan, The Rev Alexander, Minister of Daviot
Succeeded his father, the Rev William Lunan as Minister, and married Janet, daughter of Sir James Elphinstone of Logie. He died in 1731.

McGie, James
In Waterton, Aberdeenshire.

28

McGregor, Alexander
>   Younger brother of Callum McGregor in Richaharne.   Tenant of the Earl of Aboyne.

McGregor (or Gregory), Callum or Malcolm, in Richaharne (now Reinacharn)
>   Tenant of the Earl of Aboyne.   In 1696 he had three sons, Grigor, John and Archibald.

McGregor, John
>   Younger brother of Callum McGregor in Richaharne.   Tenant of the Earl of Aboyne.

McHardy, John, in Glengairn
>   Tenant of the Earl of Aboyne.   In 1696 he was married to Margaret Ochterlonie and had a son, David.

McHenry, George, Collector of Cess, Aberdeen

Mackenzie, James
>   Son of Kenneth of Dalmore, served heir to his father on 29 June 1723. In 1728 married Isobel, daughter of John Douglas of Tilquhilly, and died before 1733 leaving one child, Agnes.

Mackenzie, Kenneth, of Dalmore
>   Owner of Mar Lodge.   Married with two children.

Maitland, The Rev David, Episcopal Minister of Forgue
>   Third son of the Rev John Maitland, Minister of Inverkeithny.   It is stated he lost his sight about 1734, but continued to discharge the duties of the ministry though blind, and again recovered his sight on undergoing an operation for cataract.

Maitland, The Rev James, Minister of Inverkeithny
>   Born in 1671, he was the eldest son of the Rev John Maitland, also Minister of Inverkeithny, whom he succeeded.| He was present as Chaplain at Culloden in 1745.

Maitland, The Rev John, Minister of Forgue
>   Younger brother of the Rev James Maitland, Minister of Inverkeithny, he was ordained Minister of Insch on 26 April 1703.   He married Christian Ramsay, and died 16 April 1740, in his 69th year.

Maitland, The Rev Richard, Minister of Nigg
>   Schoolmaster at Foveran in 1671, he married three times (1) Susanna, daughter of Rev Alexander Irvine, Minister of Longside; (2) Katherine, daughter of the Rev John Milne, Minister of Fetteresso, and had issue 15 children; and (3) Mary, daughter of the Rev George Keith, Minister of Old Deer.   He died in 1719.

Marr, George, Merchant
>   On the Burgess Roll of Aberdeen in 1700.   He survived the Rising.

Martin, Peter
>   Servant to John Hamilton of Gibston, discharged from Newgate in Dec 1716.

Maule, George, Factor for the Earl of Panmure
>   Son of Patrick Maule and Christian Forbes.   Married to Susan Stuart they had James, baptized on 30 Aug 1696, Henry, baptized in 1698 and John, baptized in 1700.

Menzies, Charles, of Kinmundy

The owner of this estate in 1715.

Menzies, William, of Pitfodels

Son of Gilbert Menzies, 4th Laird of Pitfodels and Beatrix Fletcher. Born in 1688, educated at the Scots College at Douai from 1700-1707, married Mary, eldest daughter of John Urquhart of Meldrum, and had six sons, all Jacobites of '45. Died on 6 January 1780 being 92, and his wife, Mary, died 20 April 1771, aged 80.

Meston, William

Born in Midmar about 1680, son of William Meston, blacksmith and Katherine Leonard. MA degree from Marischal College, he became a Regent and appointed Professor of Philosophy in 1713, but was deposed after the Rising. He died in 1745.

Middleton, Captain Alexander

One of the fourteen sons of the Rev George Middleton, born in 1676. Married to Elspet Burnett in 1705. He died on 26 October 1751.

Middleton, The Rev George, Principal of King's College, Aberdeen

Eldest son of Dr Alexander Middleton, Principal of King's College, Aberdeen. Was baptized 25 February 1645. He married Janet Gordon, and had by her fourteen sons and four daughters! He died May 1726 in his 82nd year and his sturdy widow survived him until 1753, when she passed away at the age of 101.

Mitchell, Thomas, of Thainston

Born in 1659, he was the second son of Baillie Thomas Mitchell of Tilliegreig by his second wife, Marjory Moir. He married three times, first in 1692 to Janet, daughter of Sir Patrick Leslie of Eden, secondly Isabella, sister of Alexander Paton, afterwards Provost of Aberdeen, and thirdly Jean Mercer. He died in December 1719, leaving at least one son Thomas, who died in 1721. His only daughter was named Barbara.

Moir, Alexander, of Scotstown

Son of Dr William Moir of Scotstown and Spital who married Jean daughter of Alexander Abernethy, 1st of Mayen. He married Mary Chalmers and had two sons, William and George, and two daughters, Janet and Jean. He died in 1752.

Moir, Alexander, Regent, Marischal College, Aberdeen

Second son of John Moir, 1st of Stoneywood. In the Poll Book of 1696 it states that he had no wife, child or servants.

Moir, James, 2nd of Stoneywood

Brother of Alexander Moir, Regent. Eldest son of John Moir, 1st of Stoneywood and his wife Jean, eldest daughter of James Sandilands, 1st of Cotton. Baptized in Aberdeen, 1 Sept 1659. MP for Aberdeenshire from 1689-1707. He married twice, on 10 July 1683, Mary, eldest daughter of the Rev William Scroggie, Bishop of Argyll, issue four sons, the eldest being James, and three daughters. Secondly, Jean, daughter of Alexander Abernethy, 1st of Mayen and widow of William Moir of Scotstown. By her he had three sons, one of whom was William Moir of Lonmay, and two daughters. Jean

Abernethy died in Nov 1749 aged 85. He died on 22 Nov 1739 aged 80.

Moir, James, younger, and 3rd of Stoneywood

Son of James, 2nd of Stoneywood and his first wife, Mary Scroggie. He married Jean, daughter of William Erskine, 6th of Pittodrie, and had five sons and two daughters. It is asserted that he survived until 1782.

Moir, William, of Invernetty, Peterhead

Third son of John Moir, 1st of Stoneywood, born in 1669. Became merchant in Aberdeen. He married Christian Guthrie in 1710 and then Jean, daughter of Colonel Lewis Hay by whom he had two sons, James and William. His Will is in the Commissariot of Aberdeen for 22 Dec 1744.

Moir, William

Tenant of David Lumsden of Cushnie "forced to be in the Rebellion by the threats and force of the Earl of Mar" and taken prisoner at Preston in November 1715 with 12 other tenants of David Lumsden or Harry Lumsden of Auchindoir and Robert Reid of Mid Clove. Transported to Virginia in 1716.

Moir, William, Bursar, King's College, Aberdeen

"On Thursday, 1 February 1716 came up the street of the old towne with the picture of the Duke of Brunswick fixed behind the musle and the Ramer of his gun. He was one of those who had a gun, and who afterwards committed disorders at Alexander Taylor's house in Cotton and took away his armes."

Mowat, William, Merchant, Aberdeen

Taxer appointed by the Town of Aberdeen.

Murray, The Rev William, Minister of Inverurie

A native of the Garioch, he was at King's College, Aberdeen in 1667. He married Magdalen Gellie and had five children.

Niven, Thomas, Merchant

One of the merchants of Aberdeen from whom the Government took gunpowder to send to Edinburgh.

Ogilvie, Archibald of Rothiemay

Son of Sir Patrick Ogilvie, Lord Boyne, by his second wife, Anne Douglas of Whittinghame. Born about 1680, he married Isobel, third daughter of the Rev George Meldrum, Minister of Glass and his wife Jean Duff of Keithmore. He had sons James and Patrick and a daughter Mary. He died abroad in or before 1736.

Ogilvie, James, of Boyne

Eldest son of Sir Patrick Ogilvie of Boyne, and his first wife Anna Grant, he was born in 1667. He married in 1688, Anna, daughter of Major George Arnot of Grange in Fife, by whom he had a son James and one daughter. He married secondly, a Frenchwoman of the name Busilie, by whom he had a son, John Lewis.

Ogilvie, James, younger of Boyne

Son of James Ogilvie of Boyne and his first wife Anna Arnot. Lived mostly with his father in France, returning for the Rising. He never married, and died at Rouen in 1717.

Ogilvie, John, Bursar, King's College, Aberdeen

Expelled for seditious practices 30 April 1716. He and his brother Patrick, a year older, with William Moir, came to the house of William Walker, the Town's Drummer, and forced him to go out with his drum and make proclamation, "desiring all persons to come and see the Duke of Brunswick burnt in effigie."

Ogilvie, Patrick, Aberdeen

Ogilvie, William, Chamberlain to the Earl of Erroll

Nothing is known of his family. He was certified to be dangerously ill after Sheriffmuir, and subsequently died in Edinburgh Castle of asthma and heart failure.

Ogilvie, William, the Earl of Erroll's chamberlain

Jacobite at Fraserburgh where the town was searched for the arms left by Lord Lovat and John Forbes of Culloden. These were delivered to George Keith, younger of Ludquharn.

Oliphant, Colonel The Hon William

Third son of Patrick, 6th Lord Oliphant and his wife Mary, daughter of James Crichton of Frendraught. He married Marie Magdeleine Elinga of Frisian extraction. He had a son or sons who predeceased him, and a daughter, Marie Jean Baptiste, who was married at Orleans on 19 Nov 1710 to Louis Grenolias, sieur de Cornou.

Ord, John, of Findochty

Eldest son of William Otd of Findochty and his wife, Jean Innes. He married Elizabeth, daughter of Sir Alexander Innes of Coxton (Contract of Marriage 9 Aug 1710).

Park, Captain James, Shipmaster, Peterhead

It was in his house that the Chevalier slept the first night on his arrival in Peterhead, 22 Dec 1715. It is said that he carried the Royal Personage ashore on his back. He married in 1714, Janet, youngest daughter of Alexander Arbuthnot, Dyer in Peterhead, and widow of John Dalgarno of Mill of Rora. They had a daughter Ann. Their son was Rev Charles Cordiner, Minister of the Episcopal Church in Banff. He died on 26 May 1739 aged 59.

Paterson, Robert, Principal of Marischal College

Younger son of John, Bishop of Ross. He was married by 1696 and had eight children.

Paton, Alexander, of Kinaldie

Son of Alexander Paton, Provost, and his first wife Elizabeth Urquhart. He was a pupil in Sept 1700.

Paton, John, of Grandhome

Eldest son of George Paton, Advocate, and his wife Isabella Christie. Born in 1675, he married twice, first at Troup House on 31 Jan 1710 to Margaret, (died 6 Mar 1715) eldest daughter of Alexander Garden of Troup, and had a son, George. Secondly he married Christian, daughter of John Forbes of Leslie. He died 5 Aug 1739.

Peacock, George, Regent of Marischal College, Aberdeen

He married Elizabeth, daughter of Dr James Leslie, and is mentioned in the Poll Book (1696) with his wife and three children.

Pirie, George, Periwigmaker in Fraserburgh

A warrant had been issued for his arrest, but he was allowed bail on promising he would "carrie himself Loyally to his Majesty King George."

Pittendrigh, Robert, Merchant, Aberdeen

He had married before Aug 1715, Sophia, daughter of John Forbes of Auchanth. He survived the Rising.

Rae, James

Tenant of David Lumsden of Cushnie "forced to be in the Rebellion by the threats and force of the Earl of Mar" and taken prisoner at Preston in November 1715 with 12 other tenants of David Lumsden or Harry Lumsden of Auchindoir and Robert Reid of Mid Clove. Transported from Liverpool to Jamaica or Virginia on *Elizabeth and Anne* 29 Jun 1716, landed at York, Virginia.

Ramsay, The Rev Gilbert, Minister of Dyce

Son of Robert Ramsay, merchant of Aberdeen, at Marischal College in 1673. His wife was Jean Livingstone, by whom he had a daughter, Anna. He died 31 May 1728.

Ramsay, William

Jacobite at Fraserburgh where the town was searched for the arms left by Lord Lovat and John Forbes of Culloden. These were delivered to George Keith, younger of Ludquharn.

Reid, Alexander, Alford, Aberdeenshire

Transported from Liverpool to Maryland on *Friendship* 24 May 1716, settled Reidbourne, Chester River, Calvert County, Maryland. Died 14 Oct 1718.

Reid, The Rev John, Minister of Durris

Schoolmaster of Banchory-Ternan, he was made clerk to the Session in 1670. He married twice (1) Isabel Fraser, (2) Margaret Cruden, who survived him. He died before 2 Apr 1728.

Reid, Peter, Catholic Priest

Son of Alexander Reid and Isabella Brebner, and educated at the Scots College in Rome. He returned to Scotland in 1709 and died at Presholme in 1726.

Reid, Robert, of Mid Clova

The grandfather of Robert was the younger brother of James Reid of Bourtie, and son of Alexander of New Milne. Transported from Liverpool to to Virginia on *Elizabeth and Anne*, and still there in 1723.

Ried, William, Merchant in Aberdeen

Reid, William, Messenger

Met at Mistress Hepburn's house on 22 September (see William Hepburn).

Rickart, David, of Rickarton

Second son of George Rickart of Arnage and Auchnacant by his wife, Janet, daughter of Sir William Forbes of Monymusk. He married Katharine Arbuthnott, daughter of Robert, 2nd Viscount Arbuthnott and widow of Robert Gordon of Cluny, by whom he had one son John, and two daughters. He died 29 July 1718, aged 51.

Ritchie, Andrew, of Foresterhill

Taxer appointed by the Town of Aberdeen.

Ritchie, John, younger, Shipmaster in Fraserburgh

A warrant had been issued for his arrest, but he was allowed bail on promising he would "carrie himself Loyally to his Majesty King George."

Ritchie, Malcolm

Tenant of the Earl of Aboyne.

Robertson, The Rev Alexander, Fochabers

In September 1716 "Att Elgin. The Presbytery complained of the various encroachments made upon their ministry by Episcopal preachers, eg Alexander Robertson, who kept a meeting-house."

Robertson, The Rev Alexander, Minister of Longside

Son of Rev Thomas Robertson, Minister of Longside, was presented to Longside (as assistant and successor to his father) in 1687. He was proprietor of Downiehills, Peterhead and is mentioned as having seen a mermaid! He married Christian, daughter of John Mercer, Minister of Kinnellar, and had three sons and one daughter.

Robertson, George

Taxer for the Town of Aberdeen. Was Deacon of the Shoemakers and Convener of the Incorporated Trades in 1726 and 1727.

Robertson, James

Jacobite at Fraserburgh where the town was searched for the arms left by Lord Lovat and John Forbes of Culloden. These were delivered to George Keith, younger of Ludquham.

Robertson, The Rev John, Episcopal Minister, Strathdon

Sometime schoolmaster of Strathdon, and on 24 July 1681 was ordained Minister of that parish.

Robertson, William

Younger brother of Alexander, the Laird, and son of Rev Thomas Robertson, Minister of Longside.

Roper, Thomas, Schoolmaster of Rhynie

On his tombstone is says "Here lyes Mr Thomas Roper, who was sometime Schoolmaster at Rhynie, lawful husband to Jean Innes, who died 9 March 174-, aged 81".

Rose, The Rev Alexander, of Cairnie

Fourth son of David Rose of Earlsmill, near Darnaway (a branch of the Kilravock family). Minister of Cairnie from 1680 to 1716 when he was deposed for reading the Chevalier's Proclamation from his pulpit. Described as "courageous, firm of purpose, of good judgement, and although choleric not vindictive." He married Ann, daughter of James Gordon of Daach, and had five sons and two daughters. He lived to a great age.

Rose, Alexander, of Lethenty

Eldest son of the Rev John Rose of Insch, Minister of Foveran and his wife Isobel, dauthter of John Udny of Udny. He married Anne, daughter of Alexander Forbes of Ballogie, by whom he had three sons and four daughters.

Rose, David, Schoolmaster, Cairnie

While occupying this position he joined the Jacobite army in 1715 and went south.

Rose, John, of Allanbuie

Married Elizabeth, daughter of Alexander Gordon, 4th of Arradoul.

Rose, (or Ross), The Rev Patrick, Episcopalian Minister of Arbroath

Uncle of William Rose, Factor to James, 2nd Earl of Fife.

Ross, John, Mill of Denety

Son of Alexander Ross who was at Mill of Denety (Dinnet) in 1667.

Ross, John

Son of a Bishop or Archbishop.

Ross, Peter, tailor in Braemar

Captured by the Dutch near Burntisland 11 January 1716

Sandilands, Patrick, Sheriff-Depute of Aberdeenshire

Eldest son of Patrick Sandilands of Cotton and Margaret Ord. His wife was Barbara, daughter of William Cumine of Pitullie, but she died without issue.

Scott, Alexander, Shipmaster, Aberdeen

The Poll Book (1696) gives "Alexander Scot, Skiper for himselfe, no wife, child, nor servant; his brother, William Scot, ane boy."

Sempill, Robert, Titular Lord Sempill

Father of the Jacobite Lord Sempill

Shand, Thomas, Merchant, Aberdeen

Was probably a younger son of Thomas Shand of Craig, near Dyce, Treasurer of Aberdeen 1672-78, and his wife Anna Duncan. Married Isobel, only daughter of Thomas Hay, Sheriff-Clerk of Aberdeen. His Will is dated 1748.

Shand, William, servant to the Laird of Mayen

One of the prisoners in Stirling, taken at Sheriffmuir, which goes to show that his master was probably also present at the battle, with Huntly's Foot.

Shaw, Patrick, servant to John Abernethy of Mayen.

A prisoner at Stirling.

Shirrefs, Alexander, Drumnagour, Kildrummy

Son of James Shirrefs, farmer, of Little Miln (on the estate of Lord Forbes) and his wife, Christian Blair, living at Cornabo (probably a farm of that name in the parish of Monymusk). He married three times, but only the name of his second wife, Agnes Ferrier, is known. By his first wife he had four sons, and by his second a daughter and two sons.

Sibbald, The Rev James, Keith

In the Kirk Session Records of Keith, 1716, he is called "the Scandalous Trumpeter of Rebellion and late Preacher of the Episcopal Meeting House in the Parish."

Simpson, William, Baillie, Aberdeen

Married at Aberdeen, 11 Sept 1699, Mary, daughter of David Aedie, of Newark and Easter-Echt, Aberdeenshire and had at least one daughter, Sarah.

Sinclair, George, Merchant, Aberdeen
Taxer appointed by the Town of Aberdeen.

Sivewright, James, Westertown, Huntly

Skene, James, Captain, of Halyards, Fife
From the Aberdeenshire family. Fifth son of John Skene, 4th of Halyards, and his wife Elizabeth, second daughter of Sir Thomas Wallace, Baronet of Craigie. He married Mary Ann, daughter of the Rev J. Smith of Battersea, and died in 1736 leaving two sons and one daughter.

Smith, Alexander, Merchant
Jacobite at Fraserburgh where the town was searched for the arms left by Lord Lovat and John Forbes of Culloden. These were delivered to George Keith, younger of Ludquharn.

Smith, The Rev Alexander, Episcopal Minister, Bellie

Smith, Joram, Barber
Met at Mistress Hepburn's house on 22 September (see William Hepburn).

Smith, Patrick, Junior, of Inveramsay
Son of John Smith of Inveramsay, who died in 1750 aged nearly 100. He married on 8 November 1705, Elizabeth, daughter of Alexander Kerr of Menie, and had three sons and six daughters. He died in 1743.

Smith, Robert
Jacobite at Fraserburgh where the town was searched for the arms left by Lord Lovat and John Forbes of Culloden. These were delivered to George Keith, younger of Ludquharn.

Smith, William, Regent of Marischal College, Aberdeen
The Poll Book (1696) states that he had then "no wife, child, nor servant."

Smith, William, Merchant
Taxer appointed by the Town of Aberdeen.

Souper, William, of Gilcomiston, Merchant, Aberdeen
Son of John Souper, merchant burgess of Aberdeen, and his wife, Margaret Clark. Married in 1685, Jean, eldest daughter of James Byres of Coates, by whom he had eight sons and four daughters. Died in Aberdeen, 20 Sep 1724, aged 63.

Southest, James, 5th Earl of
Only son of Charles, 4th Earl of Southesk, and Lady Mary Maitland, second daughter of Charles, 3rd Earl of Lauderdale. He was born 4 April 1692 and succeeded when only a child of 8. He had a wife and children.

Speediman, David, Glover, Aberdeen
Convener of Trades. He was married to Christian Adamson and had at least two sons, William and James.

Spence, William, Hook-maker
In 1713, he had been Master of the Trades Hospitality Charity, also he met at Mistress Hepburn's house on 22 September (see William Hepburn).

Stewart, Andrew, of Auchlunkart

Eldest son of Patrick Stewart of Tanachie and his wife, Anna, daughter of Thomas Gordon of Myretown. Married 5 Dec 1706, Helen, daughter and heiress of Walter Innes of Auchlunkart. He died 17 Sept 1719 leaving a son, Alexander.

Stewart, Gordon

Second son of Patrick Stewart of Tanachie. Married in 1722, Anne, daughter of Sir James Abercromby, Baronet of Birkenbog, and died in Dec 1748, leaving two sons and two daughters.

Stewart, James

This was the man who supplied meal to Rannes.

Stewart, John, of Drumin

Married in 1702 to Elizabeth, daughter of George Forbes, 3rd of Skellater, and had at least two sons, Charles and Gordon. There was also one daughter, Isabella.

Stewart, John, in Ballaterach

Factor to the Earl of Aboyne, and brother of William Stewart of Aucholzie.

Stewart, John, of Boggs

Younger brother of Andrew Stewart, 4th of Tanachie. Married before 4 Nov 1697, Jean Gordon of Farskane.

Stewart, Captain John, of Dens and Crichie

Son of Colonel James Stewart, described as "of the Mearns," but of whom not much is known except hat the came of the family of Stewart of Kilcoy, Ross-shire. He married Agnes, born 1661, (died 1729), daughter of Gilbert Gray, who lived at Shivas. It is alleged that she was so plain that the Earl of Moray said he would rather pay £500 than marry her! The issue was a son, John, born in 1703, who died unmarried in 1749, and a daughter, Theodosia, born at Inverness in 1701 and died 1769. He died in 1729.

Stewart, Robert, Late Provost

Son of Alexander Stewart of Newhall, Fife, born 1670. Married Anne, daughter of John Gordon, Provost, and had two sons and four daughters. Died on 10 Mar 1749, aged 78.

Stewart, William, of Aucholzie

Married twice, first to Barbara Farquhar by whom he had a daughter; secondly to Eupham, daughter of Harry Farquharson of Whitehouse, by whom he had three sons and four daughters. He died about 1727.

Strachan, Alexander, Merchant, Aberdeen

There were several of this name in Aberdeen at the time.

Strachan, The Rev Sir James, Baronet of Thornton

Eldest son of Sir James Strachan, 3rd Baronet and his second wife, Elizabeth, third daughter of Thomas Forbes of Waterton. He married twice (1) Katherine Rose, who died in 1680; (2) in 1681, Barbara Forbes of Waterton (niece of his father's second wife). James, his eldest son, predeceased his father and is believed to have been killed during the Rising of 1715, and another brother, Francis, is stated to have followed the fortunes of the Stuarts, lived in Paris and taken Orders. Died at Inverness in 1715 aged about 75.

Strachan, Thomas, Baillie, Aberdeen

His Will is in the Commissariot 13 December 1738, with that of his daughter, Margaret.

Strachan, William

Swan, The Rev William, Minister of Pitsligo

Son of Rev Alexander Swan, Minister of Pitsligo and his first wife, Jean Leslie. Took a degree at King's College, Aberdeen in 1679. He married Grizel Robertson and had two sons, Alexander and William. In 1742 he was aged eighty-four, and died soon afterwards.

Taus, Charles

Tenant of the Earl of Aboyne.

Taylor, John

Jacobite at Fraserburgh where the town was searched for the arms left by Lord Lovat and John Forbes of Culloden. These were delivered to George Keith, younger of Ludquharn.

Thompson, Andrew

Taxer appointed by the Town of Aberdeen.

Thompson, Patrick, Under Master, Grammar School, Aberdeen

Thomson, John

Jacobite at Fraserburgh where the town was searched for the arms left by Lord Lovat and John Forbes of Culloden. These were delivered to George Keith, younger of Ludquharn.

Thomson, William

Collector of Cess at Cullen.

Tulloch, David

The very much younger half-brother of Thomas Tulloch of Tannachy, David was the fifth son of Alexander Tulloch by his second wife, Margaret Simpson.

Turner, John of Turnerhall

Eldest son of Robert Turner, 1st of Turnerhall and Margaret Rose, born in 1694. He married Margaret, daughter of Farquharson of Westone, Tarland, and had three sons and three daughters. Died in 1756.

Turner, Robert, 1st of Turnerhall

Fourth son of Andrew Turner of Kinminity in Birse. Married Margaret in 1693, eldest daughter of John Rose of Rosehill. They had nine sons and seven daughters. Died in 1741.

Tyrie, David, of Dunnydeer

Eldest son of John Tyrie of Dunnydeer and his wife, Margaret Tulloch of Tanachie, Morayshire. He married firstly Elizabeth Gordon of Rothiemay by whom he had three daughters, and secondly, Anna Menzies of Pitfodels, by whom there were three sons and two daughters. He died in 1750.

Urquhart, Colonel James

Son of Johnathan Urquhart of Cromarty and Lady Jean Graham, grand-daughter of the great Montrose. He married Anne Rollo of Powhouse, and had one daughter, Grizel. He died of face cancer in 1741.

Urquhart, Dr James, Regent of King's College, Aberdeen

Son of Dr Patrick Urquhart, Professor of Medicine.

Urquhart, John, afterwards of Craigston

The only son of James Urquhart of Knockleith and his wife, Margaret Fraser of Easter Tyrie, he was born at Knockleith in 1696. In 1737 he married, at Banff, Jean, eldest daughter of William Urquhart of Meldrum, and by her had three sons and two daughters. He died in Banff on 19 June 1756.

Urquhart, John, Waterton, Aberdeenshire

Urquhart, Dr Patrick, Professor of Medicine, King's College, Aberdeen

Fourth son of Patrick Urquhart of Lethenty, afterwards of Meldrum, and his wife, Lady Margaret Ogilvy, daughter of James, 1st Earl of Airlie. Born in 1641, he married Elizabeth, daughter of Dr Andrew Muir, by whom he had eight children. He died in 1725.

Urquhart, William, Merchant in Fraserburgh

Walker, William, Drummer in Old Aberdeen

Illiterate, and on 25 April 1716 he was a married man of approximately 68 years. (See John Ogilvie, Bursar).

Warrander, Robert, Bursar, King's College, Aberdeen

Student in 1716, who made the proclamation in February 1716 "desiring all persons to come and see the Duke of Brunswick in effigie committed to the flames."

White, The Rev George, Minister of Maryculter

Married Marion Cockburn and had three sons and two daughters. He died in 1724.

Whyte, Andrew, Merchant in Aberdeen

Taxer appointed by the Town of Aberdeen.

Whyte, James, Sen

Jacobite at Fraserburgh where the town was searched for the arms left by Lord Lovat and John Forbes of Culloden. These were delivered to George Keith, younger of Ludquharn.

Wilson, George, of Finzeauch

Son of George Wilson of Finzeauch, Burgess of Aberdeen, and Christian Robertson, his wife, he was born in 1659. He married Elizabeth Colinson, and had four sons and five daughters. He died 4 June 1725, aged 66.